The Electr

Tony Hoskins

Pitman

PITMAN PUBLISHING LIMITED
128 Long Acre, London WC2E 9AN

A Longman Group Company

First published in Great Britain 1986

British Library Cataloguing in Publication Data
Hoskins, A.
  The electronic office.
  1. Office practice.—Great Britain—Automation
  I. Title
  ‚651   HF5548.2

Text set in 10/12 pt Linotron Century Schoolbook
Printed and bound in Great Britain
at The Bath Press, Avon

ISBN 0 273 02361 6

Ephraidge A. T. Rinomhota

To Tim, Catherine and David, for whom the automated
office will be their future.

Contents

Acknowledgements

Firstly, I would like to thank my wife, without whose support and encouragement this book would have remained thoughts floating around looking for a place to settle.

Secondly, my thanks go to Vivien Fulthorpe for interpreting my handwriting and for her comments during the typing of the book.

Thanks also to my colleagues and friends at Manpower Ltd, whose words and thoughts have aided me in the development of my own views.

The author and publishers would also like to thank the following for permission to use copyright material:

A T Kearney Ltd, management consultants
Carolyn Hayman, Korda Ltd
BAT Industries
Digital Equipment Corp
Manpower Ltd
Manpower Services Commission
National Economic Development Office (NEDO)
ORBIT project—DEGW, architects; EOSYS, office systems consultants; Building Use Studies Ltd, design consultants
Hewlett Packard Ltd
Sheena Wilson, Building Use Studies Ltd

1 An introduction to the automated office

The term, 'an electronic office', is being increasingly bandied around by journalists and manufacturers alike. It is being taken as indicative of the fact that the office world is at the frontier of change. This change is regarded as the result of new technologies being introduced into an otherwise stagnant industry – the office world.

Yet, most of these dark implications are misleading. The world of the office in itself is relatively new as an *organised* institution. Equally, the tools used by the office worker have shown a history of regular change throughout the annals of the office. Lastly, the functions of the office remain the same, although the methods by which these functions are carried out are changing.

What is an office?

It is important to recognise the two prime functions of an office:

1 To facilitate the provision of information from which **decisions** can be made.

2 To **communicate** the results of those decisions to interested parties, and to **communicate** information to other bodies to enable them to make decisions.

So the twin functions are **communications**, for example sending invoices, price lists and letters and **decision making**, for example, deciding whether a company's cash flow requires additional loans, whether to buy from a particular supplier depending upon the prices quoted, and deciding how to respond to a letter from a particular company.

These two functions do not change in an electronic office, rather the communication process becomes speedier, and the decision making process can be based on fuller and more up to date information.

Having identified the two prime functions, what are the components of an office?

1 **Individuals** – whose responsibilities include the communication process and the decision making process.

2 **The equipment** – which helps to store documents (eg computers and filing cabinets), to aid communication (eg the telephone and the photocopier) and to aid decision making (eg the personal computer and the calculator).

3 **The furnishings and environment** – which help to make the office attractive and comfortable, and whose presence (or absence) can aid (or detract from) the communications and decision making processes made available by new technology.

In this guide we will look at all three components to understand their role in the electronic office and how its introduction has changed the part they play.

In particular we will try to emphasise the 'people' aspect and deglamourise the technology. After all, the equipment without the individual operating it is like a filing cabinet with its key thrown away—totally useless!

Firstly, however, let us return to an earlier comment and put in perspective the speed of change of office equipment.

How new is the office and office equipment?

Offices have existed in some form or other for as far as human history can relate, but in the very early days, the equipment used was only available to learned people.

For example, ink was developed in Egypt in 3200 BC, and paper in China in AD 105, but in neither society were those tools the property of the working classes. Instead, they were used by religious orders and academics of the day to record matters of state and of history. It is worthwhile remembering that the term 'secretary' originally meant 'keeper of secrets', and this meaning is still maintained in Government jobs such as Secretary of State or Permanent Secretary.

However, it was not until the middle of the 19th Century that both the need arose and opportunity became available for offices to represent more than one clerk and a manager.

The need arose because, with industrial mass production such as the cotton mills of northern England, there also arose a need for large scale recording of information, and large scale communications (bearing in mind, of course, that the first public post service was introduced in 1840).

The opportunity became available because the techniques of large scale production meant that the tools of the modern office could begin to be produced cheaply and in mass numbers.

This development in office employment has increased rapidly to the modern day, as shown in the following table:

Secretarial, shorthand and typing employment

Year	Total
1951	510 337
1961	663 960
1966	803 520
1971	747 400

Source: Census, England and Wales, Occupational Tables, 1951, 1961, 1971. Sample Census, Great Britain, Economic Activity Tables, 1966. Office of Population Censuses and Surveys, HMSO.

Undoubtedly, this domination of our total employment by office work will continue into the future. We will see increasing use of technology such as robots on factory production lines causing improvements in factory productivity and consequent reductions in the factory work force.

At the same time as office work has begun to dominate the total employment scene, so too have we seen a change within office work itself. This has been reflected in a shift towards unskilled office work (using tools such as word processors and electronic mail).

This change results from the introduction of new office equipment and has indeed become more marked since the beginning of the 1960s. The following table shows the dates of discovery or invention of office equipment:

3200 BC	Ink (Egypt)
105 AD	Paper (China)
1040	Moveable type (China)
1335	Mechanical clock with dial
1565	Pencil (first written reference to)
1642	Calculator
1714	Typewriter
1809	Fountain pen
1823	Computer (mechanical)
1839	Microphotography
1843	Facsimile
1876	Telephone
1888	Ballpoint pen
1899	Magnetic tape recording
1930	Automatic typewriter
1937	Xerography
1946	Computer (electronic)
1950	Transistor invented and magnetic recording materials
1964	Magnetic tape selectric typewriter Tape cartridge storage medium
1969	Magnetic card selectric typewriter Magnetic card storage medium
1970	Lexitron and 3M—first video display systems
1973	Vydec introduce first floppy diskettes
1975	Microprocessor invented
1978/9	Dedicated word processor appeared
early 1980s	Commercial applications for microcomputers, and electronic mail

Clearly the introduction of office equipment has occurred regularly over the centuries, although in the past 150 years, the speed of change has increased as advanced technologies have become available. Certainly, over the past 25 years, change has been very rapid – this is particularly the case over the past 15 years with the introduction of the components of the electronic office.

So what is the electronic office?

Let us start this section by emphasising that the best way of describing the electronic office is by using a term which is fast replacing it in common use – **office automation**. Another term is **information technology**, but this is much broader, affecting the factory, the supermarket and the home as well as the office.

So, the electronic office represents the automation of office activities using electronic processes, and in particular, miniaturisation of equipment because of the use of the silicon chip. In many respects it is this last aspect which makes the electronic office feasible both economically and physically. The technology to carry out the activities we describe as the electronic office became available with the advent of the computer in 1946 when the technology was both too costly and too extensive. Now, an IBM personal computer can provide the computing power equivalent to a mainframe computer of the early 1950s which in comparison needed a whole suite of offices to accommodate it, and cost probably 5000 times the price of today's personal computer. Figure 1 (overleaf) shows both the reduction in the cost and time of carrying out data processing operations. It shows that, since 1955, the cost of data processing, in current dollars, was dropped by a factor of over 200, while processing speed was increased by a factor of nearly 400.

Obviously, with such severe reductions in capital costs, space required, and processing time, the electronic office has become available for even the smallest of offices.

What are the components of the electronic office?

One of the important things to recognise about the equipment used in the electronic office is that it often undertakes a multitude of functions (for example, a 'dedicated' word processor can also be used for maths and record keeping). Thus, the following definition of the components, categorised by their functions, will include overlaps. The most efficient use of individual pieces of equipment is in the function for which they were designed. However, the modern office can afford neither the cost nor the space required to ensure each function is carried out by purpose-built machines. Hence the modern electronic office is characterised by multi-functionality.

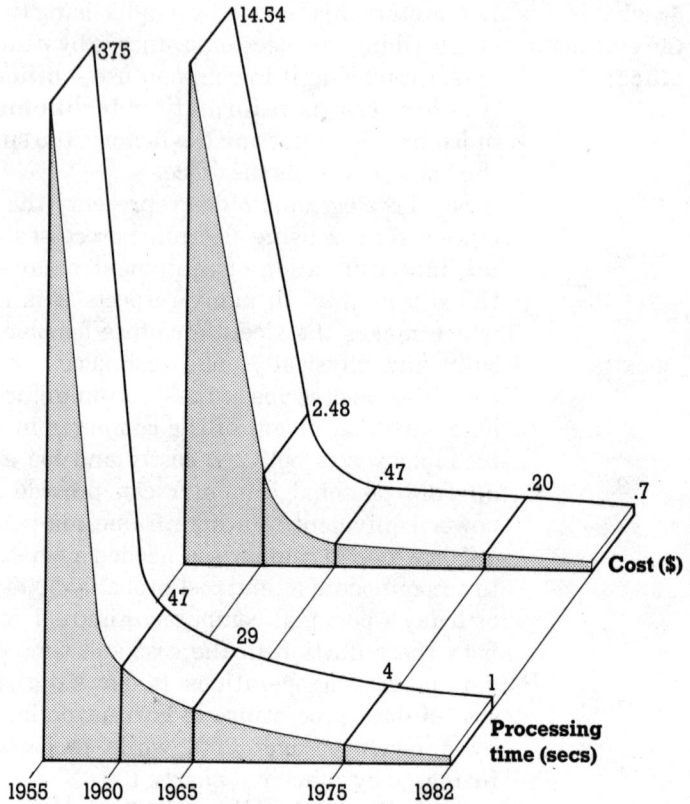

Fig 1   Cost and time to complete 1700 typical DP operations.
Source: Edwin Nixon; 'A Bright Tomorrow through Information Technology'; *The Chelwood Review*, BAT Industries

The following categorises the tools available by the uses to which they are put:

Record keeping/ filing	Mainframe computer Minicomputer Microcomputer (also known as the *personal computer*) Word processor Viewdata terminals
Communications	Telephone Electronic telex Public teletex

	Private teletex (also known as *electronic mail*)
	Local area networks (essentially the cables which connect the various pieces of equipment)
	Facsimile transmission (basically sending photocopies over the telephone links)
	Viewdata (using a central memory bank to access information)
Inputting information	Word processor
	Microcomputers
	Data entry terminals (for use with mainframe computers)
Outputting information	Printers
	Screens—otherwise known as *visual display units (VDUs)* or *cathode ray tubes (CRTs)*
Decision making aids	Management software—such as spreadsheet analysis (the most well known is probably the Lotus 1–2–3)
	Expert systems (otherwise known as *artificial intelligence*)—a product for the 1990s

If you would care to pause for a few moments, and check back to the list of inventions and discoveries, you will see that, with one important exception, all of the pieces of equipment listed above merely replace a previously invented machine by using electronics to automate the task. The electronic office represents an evolution of office equipment, not a revolution.

The exception is the expert systems, where, for the first time, a piece of office equipment not only carries out the physical function undertaken by a human being, eg writing, or communicating, but actually carries out the mental function undertaken by a human brain – but more of this later.

Let us look instead at how the introduction of office equipment changes the role of the people working in an office.

We said earlier that the secretary used to be a male profession. The change came not with the introduction of new equipment, but with the First World War. The requirement for young men to join the armed forces meant that many jobs were left unoccupied.

In particular, the women took the opportunity to take over the secretarial function. So much so, that in Britain today, of a total of about 800 000 secretaries, no more than 1% are male.

However, this picture could change over the next two decades. This is because the secretarial job is changing using advanced technology, which in itself is more glamourous – more appealing to the males – and enabling the holder of the job to carry out a wider range of tasks than has previously been the case.

If you think this is a chauvinistic statement, then be assured you're wrong. The facts are that in the schools of today, it is the boys that are taking to the microcomputers. Ask yourselves, how many females do you know, who play Space Invaders or Pac Man?

The reference to these computer games is no mistake, since it is games such as these which develop computer literacy and computer manipulation ability—the very skills required for tomorrow's office.

Why are they important? Well, essentially, because of the way the jobs are changing. Ten or twenty years ago, there was a clear structure for the average office:

- clerical staff (recording information)
- secretarial staff (helping managers to communicate information)
- managerial staff (junior, middle and senior, at each stage collating prepared information so that decisions could be taken at the appropriate level)

Now, however, we can see a change occurring in this structure. This is happening because of the availability of automated equipment which can carry out a multitude of functions on a single machine. Thus, for example, a 'secretary' can:

- input information via a keyboard, into a storage device, thus recording information for future use

- recall some or all of that information and using electronic mail communicate that information
- using management software, such as spreadsheet analysis, can reorganise the same information into a different format, either for decision making by the job holder, or for compilation into a proposal report for communication to a higher authority.

In other words, the same individual, using one piece of equipment, can encompass most, if not all, of the tasks previously undertaken by three different categories.

The electronic office is causing a blurring of the differences between various job categories. In particular, the secretarial function is capable of reaching into the junior and middle management ranks.

Why is this so? Well, think back to how we described the tasks carried out by those ranks – 'collating prepared information so that decisions could be taken at the appropriate level'. In essence, these management ranks contribute to the management task by distilling and reordering the information so that decisions can be taken. And yet, there is now equipment which can carry out these tasks (provided the person operating the machine understands what is required). Thus, these management ranks are at risk of becoming at worst obsolete, or at best merged with other job categories.

The likely job structure in ten to fifteen years time will be:

Information operators	The inputting of routine information and routine communications
Information coordinators	The users of information and the available software to enable reports to be produced and minor decisions to be taken. This category should include secretaries, personal assistants, junior managers and perhaps some middle managers

Decision making managers	Responsibilities will include making major decisions and having responsibility for numbers of staff

The implication of this job structure and the electronic office is that the hierarchy in an organisation will be flatter. There will be fewer managers but more information coordinators. The strength and reassurance for the top managers is that the minor decision making will be to a great extent automated or standardised. The systems on which the decisions have been based will have been designed to conform to corporate policies and standards and will leave less for the individual to interfere with and hence, possibly, make a mistake.

The job of the secretary could be a key one in an organisation of the future. In this respect, and relating to our earlier comments on the willingness of boys to learn computer wizardry, the secretary of today has a very short window in which to take full advantage of the opportunities offered. Let us hope they do so!

Welcome to the electronic office

Now, nearing the end of the first chapter, let us put the electronic office into perspective:

- It represents the continuing evolution of a development in office technology that has been going on for many years.
- The importance of the electronic office is in the making of such technology available to the common man (and common business) because of the low cost and small size.
- The function carried out in the office will not change, but because of the technology, the people carrying out these functions will need to adapt to the changing jobs they will be expected to do.

In this last respect, at least, the electronic office offers considerable potential for the individuals closely involved with it.

In the following chapters we will be addressing those individuals (such as yourself) with a view to explaining in more detail what the equipment does, and how it uses software, how the individual will operate in the new job structure and how the organisation will operate. Lastly, we will take a view into the future.

2 Machines and communications

'Please Mr Postman, look and see, if there's a letter for me', Sung by the Beatles (amongst others) first in 1964

This phrase from one of the well-known pop tunes of the 1960s is a useful illustration of the way in which the office world is changing. By 1990 we will get to the stage where the song could start, 'Please desk-top computer, look and see, if there's an electronic mail message for me'. It is clear that an institution as comforting as the Post Office may be fast disappearing in terms of its usefulness to the office world of today and the future.

So what are the machines and the communications systems associated with them that are changing the modern office?

The machines of the electronic office The machine side of the electronic office is usually described as **hardware**. The opposite is **software**, relating to programs etc, so called because they are stored on soft materials, such as floppy disks, tape etc.

The hardware is the physical equipment of the electronic office, and can be split into several components:

CPU	The **central processor unit** that carries out all the transactions
Memory	Internal storage which acts as a buffer to enable the CPU to carry out many transactions at the same time
Peripherals	Input, output and external storage devices

The important fact to appreciate is that these three sets of components are common to most elements of the electronic office. However, they are likely to be represented in a variety of forms, depending upon how the equipment is intended to operate within the office.

So let us look at the types of equipment you are likely to find.

The CPU and the memory

Essentially, these two components will always be found physically side by side because they operate so closely together.

The most well-known instance is the **mainframe computer**. This is the type of large computer found in large offices whose major purpose is the fast calculation of large numbers of transactions, eg the computing of invoices. Other purposes could include the holding of large records, eg the British national insurance payments are computerised using a large scale mainframe.

In the past, these large (and very expensive) machines have not been considered for any other purpose than that of large scale and fast manipulation of records and transactions. Now, however, because of their reduction in cost and size, the computer manufacturers have recognised that these machines can undertake other tasks.

The type of tasks that are being considered come under the title **distributed data processing** (**DDP**). This offers the opportunity to use the mainframe as the core of a linked network of terminals, whose functions can include:

electronic mail and calendarising
viewdata
word processing
personal computer

These functions are described more fully later in this chapter.

Each of these terminals acts as an individual workstation, at which these functions can be undertaken depending upon the organisation's and the individual's requirements.

Going down in scale from the large mainframe computer, we come to the **minicomputer** and the **microcomputer**. From the reader's point of view, the differences between these two sets of machines relate to their physical size and the number of pieces of peripheral equipment that can be attached to them (and, consequently, the functions they can carry out).

In terms of size, the minicomputer is best compared to a small filing cabinet, whilst the microcomputer can vary from the business micro – such as the IBM PC or the Apple machines – to the home micro – such as the Sinclair Spectrum or the Commodore 64.

In terms of the peripheral equipment they can accommodate, the minicomputer is nearer in function to a large scale mainframe than to a micro. The minicomputers of today can have multiple terminals, enabling them to undertake all the distributed data processing tasks described earlier. The Digital 'All-in-1' system is a very good example of DDP using a minicomputer as a base.

The difference between a mini and a mainframe in this respect relate to:

a the speed with which the machine can undertake a transaction (the bigger the memory, the more tasks that can be undertaken);

b the physical numbers of peripheral equipment that can be attached. Again, this is related to memory size, each peripheral requiring access to the memory, particularly if it is intended to run 'on-line' – hence, the more peripherals, the more buffer memory space that is required.

However, when we look at a microcomputer, the additional pieces of equipment (and hence the additional functions) that can be attached are very few, using *the micro's CPU as the core unit*. This is because the buffer memory has limited ability to act as the basis for functions such as establishing a communicating network.

This does not mean that, the micro is not able to link into an electronic mail network, but in the main this means using a *larger computer as the core unit* driving the system. In this respect, the micro is itself acting as a peripheral terminal.

Having said that the micro, as a stand-alone unit, can undertake tasks such as word processing or spreadsheet analysis.

The important fact to appreciate about the computer family – mainframe, mini and micro – is that they are general purpose machines, capable of undertaking a variety of tasks dependent upon the software used.

However, there are dedicated 'computers' whose task in the office is to undertake a limited range of activities. The best example of such a machine is probably the **word processor**, whose major purpose is the input, editing and output of text. Another example is the computerised **telex** machine, such as British Telecom's Puma and Cheetah.

Both of these pieces of equipment are good examples of the way in which the electronic office is superseding existing tools and methods with new computer based technology which not only does the existing job more efficiently but enables us to do additional jobs as well. In the case of the word processor, the previous tool is the typewriter and the additional jobs include activities such as merging standard letters with address lists or modifying reports by insertion or deletion of paragraphs. In the case of the telex, the previous tool is the paper tape telex machine, and the additional jobs include being able to send the same message to various locations automatically or recording the time that messages are received.

As we described, these are examples of machines that are *dedicated* applications of computer technology. Consequently, the hardware and the software has been purposely designed to undertake the functions required of the machine. In the past, this has meant that the machine can carry out these functions faster and more effectively than a non-dedicated computer using software packages. In addition, from the operator's point of view, because the machine is dedicated, all the keys are usually explicitly marked to identify the functions they carry out. By comparison, in a micro there will normally be either function keys, eg F1, F2, whose task will vary with each software package, or the software will recognise combinations of letters, eg QP to WordStar means certain functions such as scrolling the screen upwards continuously. Even now, that picture is changing.

Firstly, the newer micros – eg the IBM PCs, the Wang PC and the Apple Mackintosh – contain better, more efficient silicon chips, giving them more power, and providing greater memory resources. This means that, although they are not dedicated to a specific function, their power is sufficient to overcome the inefficiencies of not being purpose built machines.

Secondly, the manufacturers are planning to use the same CPU and memory, but provide purpose specific keyboards. Hence there would be a secretarial keyboard for text editing, a professional keyboard for accountancy and spreadsheet analysis, and a scientific keyboard for programming work. Thus, the micro becomes truly multifunctional.

The peripherals

So far we have been talking about the machines that do the work and how they are organised. In many instances, however, the operator need never see the actual computer.

Instead, the operator will handle the peripherals of the computer system. As individuals you are probably well acquainted with peripherals in your everyday life but, you may not have recognised them as such. The best example is that of the automatic cash dispenser seen outside so many of our banks (usually together with long queues waiting to withdraw cash). Another example is the cash till we are beginning to see in our big shops. These point of sale terminals, as they are called, are connected to a distant computer, and the shop assistant can, with a simple series of key depressions:

- register a sale
- register the item's stocknumber
- alter stock levels, resulting in a delivery of the item from the shop's warehouse
- possibly activate an order for the item if the supplier of this particular item is connected to the computer system.

This is just one aspect of what a peripheral can do – the input side. There are three types of peripherals—devices to undertake:

- input
- storage
- output

So let us look at each of these devices and understand what they are and how they work.

The input devices

These are, as the name suggests, means of entering data
or text into the computer. They vary from keyboards to
touch sensitive screens.

The most widely known input device is, of course, the
keyboard, and yet, even this can be represented in a wide
variety of functions. The most ancient of keyboards is the
punched card machine, which is operated independently
of the computer. The completed cards are then passed
through a punched card reader which is the input device
for the computer.

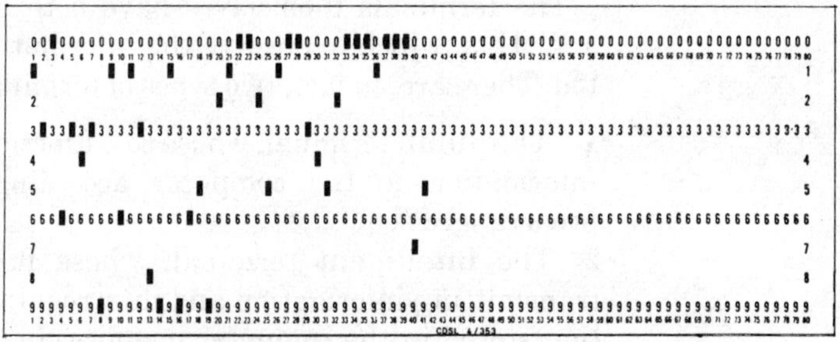

Fig 2   A punched card—the position of the hole identifies which
character or numeral is represented

It is probably fair to say that by now such machines are
almost extinct. The interesting part about punched cards
is that each column on the card represents one character
(alphabetic or numeric) and this is translated on the card
into binary code (zeros and ones) for input (see Fig 2).

Once we move past the punched card (or punched tape)
to input via a keyboard onto magnetic disk or tape, the
way in which the input device translates our information
is invisible. This is because the information is stored on
the disk in terms of electronic pulses (off and on to represent zero and one), and can only be read by using an electronic head (just like your cassette recorder uses a
magnetic head to play the music on your tapes).

Up until this stage both these methods are *remote* from
the computer, in so far as the pre-prepared input has to
be taken via the keyboard in the form of cards or magnetic

media and then read, either mechanically or electronically by an input device attached to the computer.

At this point, we come to the terminals which are connected to the computer and which enable input to be transmitted direct to the computer. This transmission can be either **on-line** – that is, the information is fed instantaneously via the keyboard into the computer (under the control of the CPU) memory – or **off-line** – that is inputting the information into a buffer memory before the appropriate time arises for transmission direct to the computer via devices that are not under the control of the CPU.

The terminals themselves have both a keyboard and a VDU on which to observe the information being inputted. There are, in fact, two types of terminal:

1 The **dumb** terminal, whose sole function is to transmit information to the computer according to a certain prearranged sequence.

2 The **intelligent** terminal, whose functions include transmitting information and interrogating the information stored in the computer memory. In this respect the terminal is capable of both transmission of data to the computer and receipt of data from it.

The intelligent terminal can vary between a machine with software designed for a dedicated purpose – for example, the inputting of quantities of items delivered to a warehouse, and the interrogation of the stock levels for items held in that warehouse – to a personal computer which can both transmit to and receive from a mainframe, and act as an independent workstation in its own right.

So far we have been talking of input devices as keyboards related, for the purpose of inputting data and text. However, we have seen the introduction of input devices which do not require keyboards.

These devices have been developed to encourage the non-keyboard literate to use the computer facilities. Some impolite observers have suggested that they are particularly attractive to managers because they can be regarded as an 'executive toy'. In fact, they are the first in a new breed of input devices. Currently there are three versions:

1 The mouse This is a small device which is connected either by wire or using infra-red to the terminal. When the 'mouse' is moved around the desk, the cursor on the screen moves in the same direction. Usually, the 'mouse' is used with a system developed by Xerox engineers at their Palo Alto laboratory. This system, as well as displaying text on the screen, also shows symbols (icons) which represent various activities. Thus, the 'mouse', by moving the cursor to an icon can instruct the computer to carry out that task with reference to the document displayed on the screen, eg moving the cursor to the icon representing a filing cabinet would cause the computer to undertake the activity 'save this file'.

2 The touch screen This system now in use with Hewlett Packard and Apple micros, avoids the need to move an independent object, such as a 'mouse'. Instead, the screen has a built-in set of touch sensitive areas, displaying a choice of activities. The user can touch one of these areas and choose to undertake that activity. At present, at least, this system, whilst avoiding the need for an additional piece of equipment, seems to be less flexible than the 'mouse', which can use more of the screen to display its icons rather than the limited touch screen area.

3 The light pen This system, at present little used by the manufacturers, could offer the best of both worlds between the 'mouse' and the 'touch screen'. It is a system whereby the light transmitted from a pen shaped instrument can activate the screen, and enable various activities to be undertaken. The successful development of this system depends upon whether or not it can be used to input text or data directly onto the screen using the light pen. Currently, it is more usually used in stock management data capture systems.

As well as these cursor or icon related 'input' devices, there are other methods which do not require keyboards:

Optical character recognition Using hand written or typed documentation, this material is 'read' by an OCR reader which then transmits them directly to the computer. This system is ideal for documents such as large quantities of standard forms. However, its weakness comes with the OCR reader's inability to read particular typefaces or handwritten insertions.

Voice recognition Very much the hope for tomorrow, and currently the subject of much research in Japan. Even today, there are voice recognition systems capable of understanding and acting upon certain words out of a special vocabulary. The research is going into how to deal with continuous speech which, if successful, could provide the means for managers to dictate direct into a word processor.

In many respects, both the printed text (OCR) and voice recognition would be the ideal input media, since there need be no third party involved in the inputting. However, until the technical problems can be solved satisfactorily, we are left with the old faithful keyboard, together with the new devices such as the 'mouse' and the 'touch screen'.

The storage devices

Once we have input the information we require, we need to ensure that there is some mechanism for retaining it in a retrievable form so that we can work on the data, perhaps the following day, or even in a year's time. To meet this need the magnetic storage devices were developed.

The most common of these devices – particularly to any of you who are acquainted with home computers – is the **tape cassette**, on which programs, data and text can be stored. However, the disadvantage of this inexpensive method is its unreliability and the very slow speed at which the computer can retrieve stored information. In addition, because the tape runs through its length, the computer cannot easily and accurately 'jump' into the middle of a tape to pick out a particular piece of information.

Consequently, there was a need to obtain reliable storage devices which were capable of operating at fast speeds and which gave the computer the ability to 'jump' into a whole range of information and read specific information immediately. This need was solved by the **floppy disks**.

These are disks of vinyl, similar in many respects to record discs, but lighter and flexible. Normally you cannot see the disk itself because it is protected by a dust jacket to prevent the stored information being destroyed accidentally.

The floppy disk works on the principle of the disk drive (the reading unit) being able to spin the disk very fast with the reader head moving in a line along the radius of the disk (the disk itself is split into many 'sectors' each of which stores separate sections of information). The movement of the head is determined by the computer which reads the index on the disk and determines where particular pieces of information are stored on the disk.

The floppy disks are portable, only requiring a disk drive to enable the information stored on the disks to be read. However, the weaknesses are twofold—their susceptibility to maltreatment by users, causing loss of stored information, and their physical limitations in terms of the amount of information that can be stored. It is worthwhile comparing the various storage capacities:

cassette tape – 250 000 characters
floppy disk   – 1 000 000 characters

Even these figures are becoming fast out of date, since manufacturers are providing double density disks, with over 2 million characters storage.

However, this level of storage capacity can be inconvenient, particularly in business applications, perhaps using large databases. For this reason, the **hard disk** or **Winchester** has been introduced. These are sealed units which are built into or alongside the microcomputer housing, and as such, are not portable. However, the strengths of hard disks are their avoidance of accidental information loss, and also the very large storage capacity – up to 26 million characters for microcomputer use, and up to 200 million characters for mainframe use.

Most microcomputers with hard disk storage also have a floppy disk drive alongside it in its housing to enable information such as software programs or updates of the database to be inputted to the computer.

The choice of storage depends upon the uses to which

the storage memory will be put, and of course, financial constraints.

Also within the computer, on the silicon chips which go to make up the CPU, there are two memory stores. These are **ROM** (read only memory) and **RAM** (random access memory). The difference between ROM and RAM is that ROM is normally related to the main memory store on the CPU in the computer and can only be read by a user program, not written to or updated. The information stored in ROM concerns how the computer operates and will be written in machine code. However, the information stored in the RAM will relate to the activity currently being undertaken by the computer. Hence this memory will store information provided by the floppy disks – data and programs, any information inputted on-line for the purposes of this particular transaction, and the results of any calculations or activities undertaken by the computer. When the activity is completed and the results outputted, the RAM will be cleared of any information stored and held ready for use in the next series of activities.

The output devices

It is in the area of output devices that the most user related developments can be seen in the hardware side of the electronic office. This is largely because, as the costs and size of the CPU have reduced, so other uses have developed for the computer and computer based equipment. Consequently, the output devices have had to be developed in great variety.

The traditional output device is the line printer. Even within the line printer, however, there have been considerable developments, which have effected quality, speed and price.

Letter quality printers

1   Daisy wheel printer   Characters are held on a circular wheel (see Fig 3). The characters can come in various typefaces and the daisy wheel can be easily changed whenever a new typeface is required. This printer requires an

ink ribbon (usually in a cartridge) against which the daisy
wheel strikes to create the character on paper.

Fig 3   A daisy wheel—one character appears on each 'petal'
of the daisy

2 The ink jet printer   Characters are created by
squirting blobs of ink onto the paper through an electrostatic field. This electrostatic field is programmed to create
different forces, thus creating different characters on the
paper. Any number of typefaces can be accommodated.
This type of printing, because of its sophistication, is
probably used as the central printer for a group of office
automation equipment and would be the responsibility
of a specialist member of staff. However, the strong benefit
is that the print is 'publication quality', (since no impres-
sions are created by striking typeface against paper).

3 The laser printers   Similar in operation and quality
to the ink jet, and apparently superseding them in the
market place because of relatively easier operation. The
laser printer creates characters by using lasers on light-
sensitive material.

The daisy wheel printer is probably the most convenient
and cheapest of these three forms of letter quality printers,

particularly since it can stand beside a stand-alone piece of office automation equipment. However, it is also the slowest, with a speed of about 50 cps (characters per second) compared with speeds of about 90 cps for the laser and ink jet printers.

Dot matrix printer

So far we have referred to letter quality printing, but the most common form of computer printer is the **dot matrix printer**. This printer actually prints individual dots, the characters are formed as a pattern of closely spaced dots.

In the early '70s, this form of printing was of poor quality, since the dots were printed in a coarse pattern. Recently, however, much progress has been made in tightening up the pattern of dots so that they are much closer together. Hence, the printed character is now much closer to that of the letter quality printer. The advantage of the dot matrix printer is its speed – up to 400 cps, depending upon the quality of the character printing and its ability to produce diagrams and graphs within the text.

With the improvement in dot matrix printing, more businesses are considering using it as a letter quality printer. However, it has still some way to go, and the ultimate decision for the choice of printer should depend upon who will be the recipient of the finished material and, of course, the available finance.

Paper feeders

In presenting the paper to the printer, there are various methods available:

1 Single sheet feed   Essentially the same approach as placing a piece of paper in a typewriter.

2 Automatic sheet feed   Using a hopper to store paper, and then automatically feeding this paper direct to the printer.

3 Sprocket feed   Using specially prepared perforated letter paper, which has sprocket holes on each side of the paper. This paper is produced in continuous sheets, and the user has to physically separate each sheet and the sprocket holes from the printed paper. This approach is particularly appropriate for large scale mailings of standard letters where automatic equipment can undertake the separation of sheets.

The screen as an output device

We have discussed hard copy as the output medium, but, of course, with the availability of VDUs, the screen itself can be an output device, particularly where the terminal is linked to a network, thus providing the opportunity for messages to be shown on the screen.

However, the screen can act as an output device *during the activity* itself. For instance, the word processor screen outputs to the user the text contained on the document he or she is using as well as information regarding items such as format status.

Recently, the screen itself has been developed to allow the user to view various activities at the same time. This is done by the use of **windows** which split the screen into sections (usually the four quarters) and the user can operate, say, on a word processing document, whilst calling up a window to show any electronic mail messages waiting, and also through another window view the data stored which may be included in the word processing document.

The screen can, of course, be monochrome (single colour against a different colour background) or full colour. Apart from the attractiveness of displaying text in various colours, the real value of full colour screens comes into play when using a **graphics facility**.

This facility enables the user to take any set of data and display it in a graphic form. Normally, the graphics software predetermines the variety of graphic approaches that can be used, and the user chooses the most appropriate. With a full colour screen, the user can highlight various parts of the graphics in different colours, thus providing more visual impact.

However, the benefits of a graphics facility is lost to a certain extent unless hard copy versions can be obtained as well as being demonstrated on the screen. The hard copy versions can be either obtained using a dot matrix printer (but without the full colour display) or using a graph plotter which has ink pens guided by the computer software instructions.

All these output devices are currently available. Undoubtedly in the future voice synthesis will be another form of output, although at present its use is limited to certain applications.

In spite of the fact that we have the benefits of all this modern office technology in our offices the functions that are undertaken are, roughly speaking, the same as those undertaken 15–20 years ago, although less expensive and faster than the same process 15–20 years ago. So if all the functions are the same now as they were then, what makes the electronic office different? The answer lies in the way in which the machines can communicate with each other, to the user's benefit. It is this area which is both dramatically new, *and* holds the key to the success of the office of the future.

The communications of the electronic office

As we saw in the introduction, the first computer was developed by Babbage in 1823 and the first electronic computer in 1946. Even at that late stage, the computer was isolated from the rest of the organisation often behind closed doors, almost as though the computer room had to be antiseptically clean like a hospital's operating theatre.

Communication by the user with the computer was *indirect* – there had to be a large department, known as the data preparation department, which took in all the paper records and translated them for input into the computer.

Just as the computer was developing, so too, on a different track, were the communications. The telephone, invented during the 1870s, was making great strides into the office world in the 1950s. Yet still, its processes were largely mechanical, particularly in the telephone exchange where the switching was by means of the rods and cogs of the old Strowger exchanges. Nevertheless, in the early 1960s, the first attempts were being made to enable the user to communicate *direct* with the computer. Often, the need for this direct communication was to enable the user to share time on a very large computer. Thus, there would be a bureau with a large computer together with lots of the bureau's clients who would communicate with the computer using a terminal from distant locations.

At this stage, the terminal would be very much like an old telex machine, which created the program and data on paper tape. This paper tape was the input source for the computer

Unfortunately, it was not that simple because communication with the computer required a telephone line and a modem. The reason for this dual requirement is that communications are sent down a telephone line via analogue wave patterns. In contrast, the computer accepts communication (input) in a digital form. Hence the need to convert one form to another using a **modem**, (**mod**ulator/**dem**odulator).

The early modems were acoustic couplers which required the telephone handset to be physically placed over a microphone/loudspeaker for the conversion to take place. Undoubtedly, the reasons for the early slow progress in developing communications for computers and the electronic office included the mechanical inefficiencies in the telephone exchanges, and also the physical execution of the task by the user. Many computer users in those early days marvelled at the opportunities offered by the communications, but were frustrated by poor telephone quality, causing programs to be lost or data files to be incompletely transmitted.

This picture has now changed considerably for three reasons:

1 For regular communications, users are able to hire a telephone line for their sole use. This is thus permanently available.

2 The new electronic office equipment has modems integrated into the equipment, requiring only a plug to be connected rather than a handset to be positioned over a microphone/loudspeaker.

3 The communications networks are changing to digital wave patterns, so that modems will not be required. The

new fibre optic cables and also the satellite communications use digital transmission.

Thus we come to the present day, where communications are not only practically possible, but also physically and financially possible because the reduction in the size of communicating equipment has coincided with the mass marketing of such equipment resulting in significant reductions in cost.

So far, we have described *how* the communications operate in the electronic office. Let us now look at *where* communications facilities offer us benefits in conjunction with computers, namely, **electronic mail**. This phrase is often taken as only representing equipment that arrived in the 1980s, but in fact it has been around for a long time (the telex is an example of electronic mail) – recent advances in technology have enabled its scope to be far broader.

Private electronic mail

It is this area that has acquired the reputation for modern technological advances. A private electronic mail system comprises:

- a mainframe or minicomputer (or more than one depending upon the size of the system)
- on-line 'intelligent' terminals, *or* connected PCs *or* word processors whose normal function is as a workstation
- a communications network linking up these terminals with the main computer. The term for such a network within one office is a **local area network**. However, for this network to function, it requires network software to ensure the messages are relayed to the right address. It is the whole package – hardware and software – which is the communications network, the leading example of which is Xerox's Ethernet

A good example of an electronic mail system is that of Digital Equipment (DEC) who use their own 'All-in-1' software and hardware throughout their organisation, with some 15 000 terminals connected up throughout the world.

As a result of this network, a DEC manager in Reading, England, can send a message instantaneously to a manager in Boston, USA. There, that manager will be able to look up his 'electronic letter box' to check how many messages have arrived, and, as soon as the US manager has accessed this particular message, there can be a 'return receipt' – the computer will notify the sender of the message that the recipient has read it.

If the UK manager wants the message – it may be anything from a memo to a large report – to be circulated to several managers, then all that is necessary is to put their addresses on the message, and the computer will automatically 'post' them.

As regards messages, the real benefit of modern electronic mail is that the system can offer text editing (word processing), calculations, spreadsheet analysis and graphic representations of figures. Consequently, the message can be the combination of text, facts gathered from a database, and graphs all put together by the user on the terminal and then transmitted directly using the electronic mail system.

In this example, if we had been undertaking the same task say, 10 years ago, we would have required a word processor to do the text, a computer to compile the facts, a graph plotter to plot the graphs and a telex to send the message text only – graphs would have been sent separately. Undoubtedly, the message would have taken longer to compile and more mistakes would have been made.

The private electronic mail system is not only important for message transmission. One of its other uses is vitally important – **diary management** (also called **calendarisation**).

For large organisations, organising a meeting between, say, 10 people can be a nightmare, and could easily occupy a day for the secretary responsible. Now, however, the electronic mail system can radically change this.

Each terminal user has to input on his or her terminal their planned appointments for as long into the future as they are planned. Then, when a meeting is being scheduled, the organiser of the meeting asks the computer to check all the individuals' diaries to check which free times are common to all. If their common free time is acceptable to the organiser, that appointment is booked, and, just like the log of messages, the individuals concerned can look at their diary log to see if any new internal appointments have been made. All this checking can be done simultaneously, so the time savings over the normal methods are immense. It not only saves the time of the organiser, but also avoids interrupting the activities of the other participants to determine the state of their diary.

Another benefit of systems such as 'All-in-1' is the provision of an electronic filing facility. This provides the individual with the ability to file any documents either originated or received by that individual.

Thus, just as in the past a secretary could have taken a hard copy of letters and memos sent out by the manager, now that secretary can electronically file such documents.

The problems of using such electronic filing systems will be similar to those of paper filing systems – namely that they need to be purged of outdated documents at regular intervals or they become unwieldly. The idea of storing disks of filed documents because 'they might come in useful at some stage' requires a positive approach.

Public electronic mail

Of course, being able to communicate more effectively internally is a great benefit, but if you still have to rely on traditional outside communications, the benefits are lessened. However, as you would expect, the major communications companies have recognised its attractions and are now offering public electronic mail systems. An idea of the number and size of these systems can be seen below:

EMS Provider	No of Mailboxes
Telecom Gold (British Telecom)	13 000
Comet (Istel)	5 000 (inc USA)
Easylink (Western Union & Cable & Wireless)	65 000 (inc USA)

Even there figures may be conservative, since the British market alone is forecast to grow fifteen-fold by 1990.

Public electronic mail acts in a similar manner to a private system, except that the network is the provider's own telephone links, and the mainframe computer is located at the provider's offices. So, when a subscriber to one of these services wants to contact another subscriber, they use their own micro or word processor to formulate the message, and establish a telephone link with the mainframe. This computer acts as the switching mechanism and also as a mailbox. So, the message could be transmitted directly, or alternatively could wait until the other subscriber dials in. One of the drawbacks currently is that the public systems are still undergoing teething problems. Also there is the question whether links between various systems are possible – ensuring that worldwide communications are available.

An example of this mailbox technique is that of the British ski firm, 'Ski Supertravel'. Its representatives at the ski resorts need to contact its headquarters with details of snow reports, medical bulletins on broken legs etc, but so too, do the representatives of all the other ski firms. Result – the telex offices at ski resorts are frequently besieged by ski firm representatives.

Ski Supertravel stole a march on its competition by giving each of its French representatives a personal computer, a modem and the telephone number for the French terminal of the Telecom Gold network. Consequently, each night, each representative can retire to his or her hotel room, set up the direct link with Telecom Gold mainframe, read the messages from head office stored in their private mailbox, and return with messages relating to their particular resorts. A system which avoids using telex operators!

Of course, just like any computer, to use these systems, private or public, each individual has to have a password – a security code to gain access to mailboxes.

Other text communication systems

Electronic mail systems, as previously described, are sophisticated applications of computer technology. Equally, there is a high cost involved in establishing the hardware for the networks, and the software for the message transmission, but there are other text communication systems which are less expensive (but probably less efficient and comprehensive).

The simplest of all is the **telex**. This has been a feature of the office for many years and most people now take it for granted, rather than recognising it as the forerunner of electronic mail. It is a teleprinter service using the public telephone lines. Its advantages are the size of its networks (in early 1980s, there were over one million subscribers throughout the world) and the fact that printed copies of the message are produced, faster and more cheaply than the equivalent telephone call. Its disadvantages are that, all too often, the mechanical nature of the system means the message received is garbled, and also that the response will need to be passed to the telex operator for transmission – the indirectness of it adds time.

Some of the disadvantages are being overcome by **teletex** (also known as **super-telex**) – providing ordinary word processors and personal computers with links to the telex network. Essentially, this is the same as the public electronic mail system, except that there is no mainframe computer in the middle to act as a mailbox, or to interrogate the diaries of its subscribers. However, problems of ensuring a 'gateway' between telex and computer systems are still to be fully overcome.

There are two other communications systems different from telex and electronic mail in that the information they transmit is far more limited in its extent, and also the ability of the receiver to respond is limited or non-existent. These two systems are **teletext** and **viewdata** (also known as **videotex**).

Teletext is an information service broadcast for reception by specially adapted TV sets. The best known examples in the UK are Ceefax and Oracle. The information is broadcast in pages, and the recipient can only choose between the pages – it is not possible to interrogate the information source.

Viewdata represents a database or an electronic library containing many pages of information. These pages can be and are usually updated from terminals. A typical application of viewdata is the television monitor in travel agents' offices. These provide the travel agent with current information regarding bookings availability and costs. The important difference between viewdata and teletext is that, with viewdata, the travel agent can make a limited communication direct with the information source. Thus, for example, having searched the electronic library for details of the most suitable flight, the travel agent can make the reservation there and then using the viewdata terminal.

There are some countries with public viewdata systems (the UK has Prestel). This approach enables subscribers to use such systems to shop from home, or transfer funds between different investment accounts.

Non-text communication systems

Using a telex to communicate has the disadvantage that, for example, drawings of designs cannot be included in the message request. This need can be overcome by the use of **facsimile transmission (FAX)**. This looks similar to a photocopier, and is, in fact, a telecopier. To operate, it requires a telecommunications link, with two machines, one switched to 'send' and the other to 'receive'. The document to be transmitted is inserted into the 'send' machine and a copy is produced on the 'receive' machine. Undoubtedly, the speed of the other systems meant that fax has been slow to develop. Now, however, a page can be transmitted across the world in 30 seconds, and, consequently, fax has been the subject of renewed interest.

Of course being able to transmit diagrams complements much to a telex, but we must not forget that being able to communicate direct adds greatly to individuals' understanding of what each other requires. So, the **telephone** – that traditional device of the office – has been updated to give more and more facilities. Modern telephones, using computer controlled PABXs, are easing communications by providing a repeat dial capability. Equally, a user can redirect their phone calls to any other part of the building where they might be visiting. Not only this, but the management can analyse usage and costs, right down to individual extensions.

What these improvements have done, is to make using the telephone more efficient, but the greatest improvements involve the use of **conferencing**. By this, various individuals can join together for a discussion on a particular subject, even though two may be in the USA and two in Europe. **Audio conferencing** is now a common addition to a computerised PABX system. **Video conferenc-**

ing is possible although, as you would expect, it requires individuals to sit at specific positions in a studio before a camera, and therefore it cannot be an impromptu discussion. The future of video conferencing will depend very much on developments in the technology to make it easier and more flexible to use.

We have discussed the aspects of machines and their communications in the electronic office. Our assumption has been that the appropriate software is provided. Yet this is an oft-repeated mistake – because, just like the chicken and the egg, the question of which should come first, the hardware or the software, is one which should present the reader with difficulties. In the next chapter, we will review the choice of software, and the facilities available.

3 The choice of Software and the Facilities offered

We concluded the last chapter with the question: the hardware or the software, which should be chosen first? Unfortunately for the readers little help is provided if they are thinking of installing an automated office system.

If they ask the question of the manufacturers, undoubtedly they would answer the hardware, because that would be to their benefit and also because choice of software first could restrict the choice of hardware. A good example of this is the word processing system, Displaywrite 2, which has been written by IBM only to operate on their personal computer. Similarly, the very popular Lotus 123 spreadsheet and database package was limited to the PC for a great deal of its life. Obviously, if the question was asked of software houses, the answer should be the reverse, for basically similar reasons.

The important point for the reader to recognise is that their starting point should not be 'which hardware or software', but at a more basic level, 'what is my problem and what are my constraints?'

Having determined that basic question (although often not as easy as it sounds), you are then in a position to select the type of software packages to meet your needs, identify which machines are available to run them and which suit you best.

In this Chapter, we will try to make the oceans of software packages more intelligible to the layman by identifying the three basic categories into which they fall and then discussing the facilities that are commonly available from applications software. Lastly, we will try to come back to the question of choosing specific software for your office applications and give you some pretty basic tips to help you.

The three software categories

Undoubtedly, for those of you who have experienced software from the standpoint of the home computer, the fact that there is more than one type of software will come as something of a surprise, because most people who have dabbled in home computing regard 'software' as representing the applications packages – games such as Pac Man.

However, when you get into the software applicable to the electronic office, the categories of software become more readily apparent:

- operating systems
- communications systems
- applications packages

Operating systems

This software represents the instructions to tell the computer how to work. The best analogy is the human brain. This brain (the computer operating system) is capable of telling its 'mechanical' parts, such as the arms and legs, when to move (the peripherals such as disk drive, screen, etc) and also coordinates activity of the various parts of the body, such as raising a cup to the lips (arranging for particular files to be stored in particular places in the RAM). In other words, the operating system:

- manages all the hardware
- acts as a user interface and provides user facilities, such as 'talking' to the computer to *list* all file names on the disk in drive A and *retrieve* files from the disk and place in the memory

Without the operating software, the applications software cannot operate.

For those of you used to dedicated stand-alone word processors you would already be used to operating software where the disks are placed in the disk drive and read at the start up of the machine. However, if you are lucky enough to have used a multiple workstation system, you may not even have realised that there was operating software because every time you used it, you went straight into the applications software. In the latter case, the operations software was 'transparent' to the user.

With the dedicated word processors, most users will regard the software as being the 'IBM operating' software or the 'Wang operating disks'. Often this software is written specifically for this particular machine.

When we come to micros, and larger computers, however, the operating software tends to be that designed for use by a variety of micros. As a result, there are many different types of operating software, each of which has different operating criteria. A few of the better known, more important types of software are listed below:

CP/M	The first (and hence, largest used) industry standard 8-bit operating system
MS–DOS	The first 16-bit operating system
PC–DOS	The IBM PC version of MS–DOS
Concurrent CP/M–86	A 16 bit version of CP/M but one that enables the machine to do more than one job at the same time
UNIX	Regarded as the leading multi-user operating system, with the ability to link many terminals to one processor. Currently, being reviewed by many computer manufacturers to see how it can be more 'user friendly'. Could be the operating system for the 1990s

These four operating systems are only a selection – there are many more, let alone the systems from those companies who have designed their own machine specific systems.

From the reader's point of view, there are 3 points to recognise when choosing operating systems:

1 Different systems do different jobs more or less efficiently. For example, CP/M is not appropriate to multi-users, whilst UNIX, currently at least, is a system which is capable of a variety of tasks and which if required to do a simple, specific task would probably be over-sophisticated for it.

2 Each system is being regularly updated – so the CP/M version 3.0 is now available, and data disks need to be formatted to the appropriate version (otherwise they can default).

3   Applications software is written for specific operating systems. Hence, the older and more widely used operating systems will have more applications packages available. Consequently, the user has more choice. This does not necessarily mean that the user will suffer – the applications software available for say UNIX, may easily meet the user's needs – but nevertheless, it does make the job of getting an exact fit between requirements and applications software characteristics that little bit more difficult.

Communi-
cations
systems

Undoubtedly, the most challenging task to office automation equipment manufacturers is how to design the equipment and the systems to handle communications between a variety of machines. In many respects, our earlier reference to UNIX was to an operations system with a communications facility (it handles multi-users from a single processor). However, the communications systems that are vital are those that will control electronic mail within a network, and thus ensure that the network directory is used to make certain the right users get the right messages.

Because the investment is so significant to establish a user network, most computer manufacturers have developed their own communications operating systems. IBM have DISOSS, Xerox has Ethernet, and Digital has DECNet.

Fundamental to each communications operating system is an **architecture** which defines how messages of data and text are communicated between various machines. Each of these architectures seems to fall foul of the computer industry's tendency to bring everything down to initials – so that DEC architecture is called DNA, IBM's versions are called SNA, SNADS DIA.

Their most important task is to ensure one message looks exactly the same when communicated from a word processor, passed through the control computer, and delivered to the recipient on a personal computer. There is little point in being able to communicate if there is no system architecture, and thus the message entered as 'Hi, Joe, see me for lunch' becomes 'Ihj, Eos, meee of rchlun' – or words to that effect!

The good news for you, as the potential user of such communications systems, is that they are intended to be completely 'transparent'. You will never know there are communications programs beavering away to deliver the message in the right spot at the right time. Equally, these systems are more likely to be used when there are large numbers of terminals in a large organisation.

Applications packages

An applications package is a program or group of programs designed to enable the user to undertake a specific task. There are two types of applications package:

1   Those you write yourself (or have your in-house programmer write for you). These are custom built to meet your needs.
2   Those that are bought in applications packages, and which, in all likelihood, will require you to compromise on your requirements to some extent.

On most occasions, the value of having the perfect system is not worth the extra effort in doing it yourself or in-house.

Firstly, to do it yourself assumes the procedures you follow currently in-house are the most efficient means of tackling the problem. They may not be, and by computerising them you may be compounding their inefficiencies. At least with a bought-in package you have the opportunity to review how you carry out your activities.

Secondly, all tasks change whether from internal or external causes. Doing it yourself means you have the responsibility of updating – an onerous task.

For each specific task, say, word processing, there are many different applications packages. One recent survey showed there are over 50 word processing packages. Again, the differences between them will relate to factors such as:

- speed of operation
- facilties available within the program, for instance, a spelling verifier
- methods of presenting output

The user in choosing the applications software needs to have a good view of their own requirements and constraints, so as to choose what is relevant in each software package and what is superfluous to their needs.

The types of applications packages available

Within the electronic office, the number of types or categories of applications packages is very limited. Obviously, if the activities of the office overlap into other areas, for instance, production control, or scientific programming, then the numbers would expand, but basically there are five office automation categories and three traditional computing areas:

Office automation:
  word processing
  electronic mail
  graphics
  data base management
  spreadsheet analysis

Traditional computing:
  payroll
  accounts ledgers
  stock control

By making this split, it does not mean that the traditional computing areas are not changing – on the contrary, they are being affected organisationally by the impact of the electronic office. Indeed the information gathered in the traditional computing areas is used by some of the new office automation categories, and, as a consequence, causing a changed attitude to how the systems are best organised.

However, for the purposes of this view, we will only look at the new office automation categories to identify what they are and the facilities offered.

Word processing

Perhaps the traditional starting point for the electronic office. Using dedicated stand-alone equipment, word processing was gradually extended into micros, and also provided for on the large mainframe installations with multiple workstations. Word processing has extended beyond the accepted text editing to other additional facilities which make the whole software package more attractive to the user.

One of these add-ons has been referred to already – the **spelling verifier**. This is a dictionary held in the machine's memory store against which each typed in word can be checked. If the typed in word does not tally with any of the words in the dictionary, then the machine highlights that word as an exception. Of course, if the operator types in, for instance, 'tied' when meaning 'tide', there is no way the verifier can identify the error. The verifier does not check for context, only for spelling accuracy. You can include, of course, any words or names regularly used by the operator (perhaps technical words) so that these, too, can be checked for spelling accuracy. This add-on, however, is a relatively small element compared with offerings such as IBM's Reportpak designed to aid the word processor operator to generate reports using data and text combined; and Chartpak designed to enable the operator to use data to produce charts for use within reports or text. These two systems are purpose built add-ons to enhance the existing system which is usually already very extensive. Most software packages cover the applications listed in the table on pages 42–3 reproduced by kind permission of Manpower Limited.

The question facing the word processing user is 'which route should I take: dedicated word processor or micro-based packages?' Indeed, many individuals have already concluded that now there is a great variety of micro word processing software, the dedicated word processor is already dead. However, this is not likely to be the case.

Like transport, you would not want to use a car to ship a load of timber – you would use an estate car if the load was small enough, or even hire a van or a truck if the load required it. So, too, with word processing.

If the projected use of the word processor is heavy, with extensive applications of intermediate and advanced functions, then a dedicated word processor is required. Alternatively, if the word processing is part of a wide range of activities, most of which are computer related, then a micro with a variety of packages including word processing is more appropriate.

APPLICATIONS (DOCUMENTS)	FUNCTIONS USED TO PRODUCE THESE DOCUMENTS	DESIRED PROFICIENCY LEVEL B = BASIC I = INTERMEDIATE A = ADVANCED
LETTERS/MEMOS		
ORIGINAL, ONE-OF-A-KIND LETTERS	Formatting, keyboarding, making minor corrections or changes and printing.	B
FORM LETTERS WITH STOP CODES	Filling in blanks of prepared letters by keying in names, addresses, dates, etc. (Examples: past due notices, account status letters, etc.)	B
STANDARD LETTERS, MERGED WITH INFORMATION	Filling in pre-stored master letter by automatically merging with names, addresses and other variable information. (Examples: personnel reply letters, customer service reply letters, etc.)	A
STANDARD LETTERS, **SELECTIVELY** MERGED WITH INFORMATION	Filling in pre-stored master letter by **selectively** retrieving names, addresses, and other variable information from files and merging with the master. (Examples: volume mailings to selected recipients ie prospects, customers, suppliers, etc.)	A
FORMS		
PRE-PREPARED FORMS	Retrieving form format, displaying, formatting, filling in blanks by keying in variable information and printing. (Examples: insurance claims, purchase orders, etc.)	B
NEW FORMS	Creating forms on visual display by keyboarding and formatting. (Examples: report forms, applicant logs, etc.)	I
SPECIAL FORMS	Creating forms on visual display by using special software packages. (Examples: statistical tables, financial reports, etc.)	A

A classification of word processing applications

APPLICATIONS (DOCUMENTS)	FUNCTIONS USED TO PRODUCE THESE DOCUMENTS	DESIRED PROFICIENCY LEVEL B = BASIC I = INTERMEDIATE A = ADVANCED
STATISTICAL DOCUMENTS		
ANNUAL REPORTS	Formatting, keyboarding, storing, inserting, deleting, moving columns, centering column headings over columns, retrieving information, and printing. (Examples: profit and loss statements, balance sheets, etc.)	I
FINANCIAL/STATISTICAL CHARTS AND TABLES	Formatting, keyboarding, storing, inserting, deleting, moving columns, centering column headings, executing math functions to perform row and column totals and printing. (Examples: sales forecasts, budgets, etc.)	A
RECORDS/LIST PROCESSING		
PRODUCT AND PRICE LISTS	Formatting, keyboarding, storing, making minor corrections, retrieving and printing.	B
DIRECTORIES/EMPLOYEE LISTS	Formatting, keyboarding, editing, retrieving, printing, plus sorting the file and/or selectively retrieving items from files. This could also include rearranging columns to produce reports.	A
MULTI-PAGE DOCUMENTS		
REPORTS	Formatting, keyboarding, making minor corrections retrieving and printing.	B
ASSEMBLED DOCUMENTS	Retrieving, reformatting, editing, keyboarding and printing new documents assembled from blocks of stored text. (Examples: contracts, wills, proposals, etc.)	I
PROPOSALS AND STUDIES	Formatting, keyboarding, making heavy revisions including bulk moving, copying, deleting, paginating/repaginating, page numbering, headers and footers, retrieving and printing. (Often includes numerical listings.)	I
MANUALS AND HANDBOOKS (DUAL COLUMN)	Formatting, keyboarding, major revising and printing text utilising a dual column format.	A

The basic differences between a dedicated word processor and a general purpose micro are:

1   Speed of response (a dedicated machine, because its system will have been designed around that particular use).

2   Ease of use (a dedicated machine will have keys clearly identified by purpose. A non-dedicated machine will either use function keys whose purpose changes with each software program, or, as with WordStar, will use combinations of keyboard letters to achieve, say, the movement of the cursor).

As always, it is fitness for purpose that will count in the choice of the type of machine or software.

Electronic mail

Largely, these software packages are sold as machine specific by the manufacturers involved. Even so, brand names are beginning to vary, from IBM's 'Personal Services' to DEC's 'All-in-1'.

Whilst the names help to confuse, their functions are pretty much the same:

- message sending and receiving electronically
- messages filed electronically for subsequent referral
- diary management, enabling each user to interrogate other individuals' diaries to check when they would be available
- communication externally with other message systems, eg public electronic mail systems or teletex

Whilst most systems are manufacturer produced for specific machines, there are systems available commercially from software houses – an example is the Office UNIX system developed in February 1984 for the IBM PC (9 months before IBM announced their own product). In the case of Office UNIX, the communications package is called FUSION, based on Ethernet. However, this is a system developed for a particular machine, and until all machines conform to a single communications standard, there will remain a difficulty in communicating between machines of different types.

Graphics

Graphics packages have been expanding over the recent past – particularly with the availability of 4-colour screens to display the graphics.

Some individuals think of graphics packages as merely acting as a support for the manufacturer's salesperson to demonstrate the glamorous side of the machines. Whilst this may be true, in reality graphics can add very much to the strength of understanding by the reader of any report.

Graphics software usually covers several alternative presentation methods such as:

- pie charts
- bar charts
- line graphs

Inevitably the main uses for such presentations are for inclusion in business reports to make those reports more readable (and usually intelligible). However, because the graphics can be developed by the operator on the screen, the user can use the graphics packages to interrogate the data files, and by 'painting' the graphs on the screen can readily appreciate the trends in any set of figures.

One of the interesting ways in which graphics operates is with the use of the **mouse** or **icons**. The **mouse** is a touch sensitive device which enables remote control of the cursor positioning. The **icons** are representations on the screen of various activities – for example, graphics would be represented as a series of alternative graphic treatments.

The application of the 'mouse' and 'icons' to graphics software has greatly enhanced its utilisation, because the user is able to alter the style, content or presentation of the graph by moving the cursor between various 'icons'.

Figure 4 illustrates the 'icons' on the left-hand side of the screen which govern aspects such as the size of the border around the graph, the scales on the axes, the legend

in the box on the graph, whether or not the space below
each line should be colour-filled. Fig 5 shows the screen
of another machine and the variety of graphics available
for that machine.

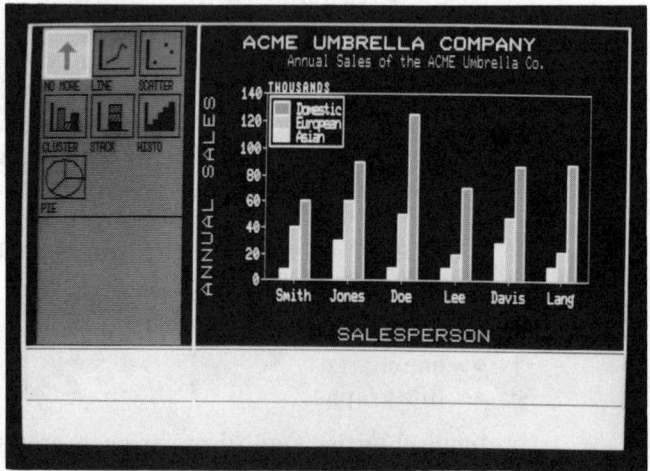

Fig 4   Graphics on the DEC All-in-1 system

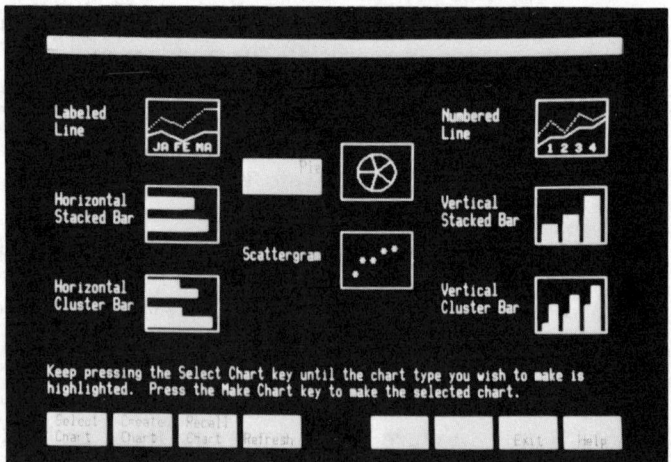

Fig 5   Graphics on the Hewlett Packard micro

Data base management and spreadsheet analysis

These two functions are becoming increasingly popular software packages for use by the executives, on their micros, or personal computer workstations. The reason is, of course, that now at last, the executives can manipulate the information themselves, rather than rely on the mainframe computer to produce it for them in a packaged presentation.

Largely speaking, these two software packages are intermingled using the same data, so much so, that some software packages actually sell on the basis of being an integrated package. Lotus 1-2-3 is such a case (the 1-2-3 means that it offers data base, spreadsheet analysis and graphics). So, too, in Multiplan. However, there are many good non-integrated packages – Visicalc and Supercalc are examples of spreadsheet, whilst DMS and dBase II are examples of database management.

The functions of each are as follows:

Database management These software packages enable a user to order or rank data in different ways – perhaps alphabetically, by class of product, or by value of sales, and then in ascending or descending order. In addition to this sorting facility, database systems offer a 'query' facility – selecting all salesmen who have sold over £100 000 of goods this year, all salesmen whose surnames begin with L, or all those salesmen who operate in Greater London.

By using this ranking and 'query' facilities an executive can quickly search the data for specific characteristics or rank the data to carry out a pareto analysis (this checks whether 80% of, say, the debts outstanding, are represented by 20% of the debtors).

Spreadsheet analysis The basic difference between spreadsheet and database is that spreadsheet offers a calculation facility, whereas database, with the exception of a totalling facility, does not.

It is best to regard spreadsheets as a screen-based representation of a sheet of accounting paper. There are columns for identifying the activities and the ledger to which it should be posted.

However, thinking of it purely as an accounting tool underestimates the usefulness of spreadsheets. Not only are you able to do additions across the columns (so, for example, if you had inputted the weekly sales for each of 100 branches, you could calculate the monthly sales by asking the computer to add columns 1–4, 5–8 etc), but also to undertake sensitivity 'what if?' analyses.

A good example of this is where an executive has set up on spreadsheet the plan for all divisions, with the following column headings:

Cost price
Recommended retail price
Discounts for bulk
Sales volumes and values
Distribution costs for volume ranges
Sales staff numbers
Staff salary and commission
Office overheads
Profit/loss

If something fundamental changes the plans after one month, and the plan needs to be revised, all the executive needs to do is to take that particular column, multiply the column by the necessary factor, and not only will the cost price changes be calculated but all the other columns will be revised and, in particular, the new profit and loss, will be calculated.

However, the example just given may relate to a reworking of a plan or a budget because of externally produced changes. What happens if the executives themselves want to consider making changes – for instance, changing the sales price or the discount structure (or both)? This type of 'what if?' analysis is relatively easy to accommodate in spreadsheet analysis.

This type of software package is important because it gives the executive control over how the information is manipulated – particularly now that information held on the mainframe can be down-loaded for use on personal computers.

Some basic tips for choosing specific software

As stated at the beginning of this Chapter, these are only basic guidelines. We are not intending to compare different software packages for the same application but only to aid you in your own decision process:

1 Know your problem – spend time thinking about what you want to solve with the software now and in the future.

2 Know your constraints – your information may not be available in precisely the right form for your program – does this difference matter (to the program or to you)?

3 Know your plans for the future – will the program need to support multi-users? Will you be planning to integrate text and data? Can your software packages do this adequately?

4 Recognise that some software systems come complete, some, such as the IBM Displaywriter Textpacks 2, 4 and 6 come in modules. Decide what level of 'skill' you want the software to have.

5 Know your operators – are they experienced, perhaps preferring a command driven software, or inexperienced using menu driven software? Decide how 'user friendly' you want to go (there is usually a compromise in terms of speed of response of the machine). Wherever possible and appropriate, involve the operators in the choice of software.

6 Check whether the existing use of other software systems within your organisation means you would benefit from purchasing the same software and perhaps being able to transfer data files. *Do not* get a new package just because you want to show your advanced knowledge.

7 Do take your time with the dealers and get a good demonstration of the system, covering *your* points and not theirs.

8 Before you buy, ask for a list of users in the same area, and go and ask them for their opinions.

9 Unless you are a computer wizard, buy ready made packages and accept they are likely to require some compromises.

10 Look at any published reviews and if you have any sense, purchase a day's consultancy from a computer con-

sultancy, and ask them to review the differences between
different packages for the same application – it will save
you money in the long run.

11   If you have made a mistake, do not try to soldier on.
You will find it frustrating and in the end more costly
than starting a fresh approach with a new software package.

By the end of this checklist, you should be ready to start
choosing your software and its hardware.

The question we should be asking is where the software
and the electronic office will lead the individuals and the
organisations themselves. The next two chapters will
show how the electronic office will affect these two parties
in the future.

4 'People make the world go around'–The role of people in the automated office

So where will the automated office lead the individual? Are we all going to be faced with robots everywhere? Or will office automation cause all of us to become automatons, doing everyday routine tasks? At the same time, will there be more or less jobs available as a result of office automation?

All these questions assume that at some stage there will be a 'big bang', and the world will suddenly change to office automation. That, of course, is not the case – it is an evolutionary development rather than a sudden revolution.

So, with that in mind, let us take a look at how jobs have changed, are changing and will change.

Pre-Office automation jobs (early 1970s)

About 10 years ago, office automation was regarded as computerisation and its impact was felt largely in the data preparation area. Consequently, the typical structure of an office fell into three categories – clerical, secretarial and managerial.

Clerical functions

Large numbers of clerks preparing information manually on standard forms for ease of input by data entry operators (such as punch card operators, or VDU operators). There were two clear aspects of the data work – data preparation and data entry. In addition, the clerical area was responsible for manual filing of paper such as invoices, customer letters etc.

These clerical operations were developed in the days when 'big was beautiful', so the numbers in one department could represent several hundred. This truly was the 'paper factory'.

Secretarial functions

Split between secretaries and typists, these were either related to the large departments, eg invoice typing, or customer letter copy typing; or associated with one or two managers. The typing role represented the next step up from the clerical role and many of the latter graduated to it by taking on typing training.

The secretarial role was clearly more that of a support to a particular manager. They processed all the manager's correspondence and reports, and organised meetings. They seldom had a great input into the manager's own activities eg providing analyses for reports, remaining the individual who took the analysis and a report and put it into good typed shape. In addition, because the secretaries worked for a maximum of two bosses, they often had the job of assisting the boss with some of his personal matters, eg typing personal letters etc.

Neither the secretary nor the typist used electronics – the most impressive technological piece of equipment they used was the IBM electric typewriter with proportional letter spacing.

Managerial functions

Here there was relatively clear delineation between senior, middle and junior management (even to the extent of their having different eating areas at lunchtimes).

Few, if any managers at any level, used electronic equipment, so the role of each level included both management of people activity and processing of information activity. For example, a company considering investing in a new piece of production plant, costing perhaps £1 million, would require some form of appraisal and investigation of the investment. The junior managers would be asked to pull together all the raw data – usually by asking their staff to manually extract it from files of information available. The middle managers, who may be proposing the project, would have identified the information they required from the junior managers and after receiving the raw data would prepare it in a report, analysing the financial pros and cons. This report would then be presented to the senior management, who would review the proposal against other competing requirements for funds, and compare its effects with what they want their organisation to achieve. At the end of this review, they would either request more information, or accept or reject the proposal.

Thus in the pre-office automation era, we had three job categories:

- **clerical** – whose role was to prepare information
- **managerial** – whose role was to analyse the information
- **secretarial** – whose role was to support the managers

These roles are now changing.

Current automated office jobs (early 1980s)

If the early 1970s was regarded as the era of computerisation, then the early 1980s will be regarded as the era of word processing. For that is what many people currently regard office automation to be.

This change, together with other changes in the data preparation side, has meant that the impact at this stage is felt mainly on the secretarial and clerical functions.

Clerical functions

The changes in this area covered both data preparation and data entry. The most significant of these was the ability for an individual to communicate directly with the computer.

Thus, on the data entry side, instead of producing punched cards or magnetic tape or disks, for subsequent input to the computer, the data entry operators were now using dumb terminals (where the operator can only input data) or intelligent terminals (where the operator can input and interrogate the computer). These terminals provided direct access to the computer, and particularly where the intelligent terminals were concerned, enabled the data entry operators to undertake a wider range of clerical tasks, since they could access files and provide information such as the customer's state of indebtedness, or shipment progress or items ordered.

The real impact of this change in computer technology came when it was appreciated that it could be applied to data preparation rather than just the data entry. So, instead of preparing the data by inputting in standard forms for entry by data entry operators, it became possible to input directly into the computer.

An interesting example of this is that of one of Britain's largest record companies whose peak days within the working week are Monday, when the shops phone in to stock up after the weekend's sales, and Tuesday afternoon and Wednesday, when the shops ring up to order records featured in the charts announced at midday on Tuesday. Previously, this had been a heavily clerical intensive task involving orders received clerks and data entry staff, thereby reducing speed and efficiency. Now, the orders are taken over the telephone by a VDU operator who inputs them directly into the computer. The order is taken and placed on the order schedule in less than a minute, enabling the record company to ensure its customers are kept fully supplied with all the most popular records.

Another example of the impact of computerisation is that of Manpower in the UK. With a large number of clients – approximately 20 000 – and a high weekly cash flow (to pay its temporaries on time), Manpower recognised that its credit control procedures were vital to maintaining a profitable company. The introduction of computerisation into that area increased its efficiency. Now, whenever a branch has a new client, it rings the staff in the credit control department, who, using interactive terminals, interrogate the computer to find out whether any business has ever been done with that client anywhere in the UK. This enables the credit control department to give a credit rating or credit limit immediately for any company.

The most important part of the computerisation deals with their cash collection, because, when clients take too long to pay invoices, the cash collection side of the credit control department uses the computer to provide information on each account (invoice date, number and amount etc) and uses this 'live' information as a source when telephoning the clients regarding earlier payments.

This whole department is computerised – a far cry from the late 1970s when such a procedure required access to heavy files of computer paper, making the task long and

arduous, and the performance of the credit control department less efficient in terms of days debts outstanding and
bad debts suffered.

Thus in the clerical area, we are beginning to see a
coming together of the data preparation and data entry
roles, with direct access to the computer using interactive
terminals as the key to this process.

Secretarial functions

It is this area which has been the beneficiary of the impact
of word processing. This in itself has increased the productivity of a secretary or typist and together with other factors such as the increasing cost of office rents, has caused
management to seek more effective utilisation of secretarial resources.

As a result, the number of managers supported by each
secretary has increased from one or two in the early 70s
to four in the early 80s.* This has meant the secretary's
role has changed to become far more task orientated –
analysing budgets, processing reports, typing letters –
than supporting managers in their total range of tasks.

Word processors and, where appropriate, microcomputers, have aided secretaries in that change. The range
of functions they can undertake include text editing, preparing standard letters, undertaking calculations and
records management. The first two examples represent
a more efficient means of continuing with a secretary's
primary task, correspondence, whilst the second two
represent an extension of the secretary's role into more
administration on behalf of the manager. This extension
is necessary as more managers are supported by a single
secretary – who often becomes a departmental secretary,
responsible for monitoring, say, departmental expendi-
ture or budgets.

This development of the secretarial role is a sign for
the future, and in many respects secretaries should take
every advantage of the opportunities offered by the change
since they are provided with the ability to gain power

* Silverstone & Towler: *Secretarial Work in Central London 1970–1981*,
published by Manpower Services Commission.

and importance within their department and organisation.

In the typing area, the typist's role has become that of the word processor operator, particularly where the use of standard letters or standard paragraphs are involved. Generally, the role of the copy typist or the invoice typist has not changed – although the equipment they use has.

It seems clear that in the future, the gap between the secretary and the typist will widen, since the typist will use a similar piece of equipment to the secretary but will use far fewer of the functions available. Thus, even at this stage, we can see the secretary's role becoming broader, providing the opportunity to manage their own tasks and spend more time solving relevant problems whilst the typist will spend more time on routine work.

For those organisations with typing pools, the introduction of word processing has had an impact on the role of the typing supervisor, who has become the word processing supervisor. This new role provides more opportunity to manage the work process – monitoring the amount of work in hand and completed – and the impact of technology on the work area.

The machines themselves, if linked to the supervisor's desk, can provide information about productivity, thus making the supervision of people a relatively easier task to accomplish. This also enables the supervisor to spend more time with the authors of the work—thus enabling their own proficiency in writing text and reports to be improved. Additionally, the supervisors are able to spend more time in identifying training needs for the staff reporting to them.

Managerial functions
In many respects the managerial area has not been affected by the introduction of technology such as word processing. Only the more specialised areas – advertising copywriters, or computer professionals – have taken to using word processors directly.

Undoubtedly, the fact there are fewer secretaries available for any group of managers has meant that managers must change their use of secretarial resources. For instance, where appropriate, they have standardised sales letters containing standard paragraphs. However, these changes are few – in fact one of the big problems of the current office automation scene is that too few managers have a full appreciation of the impact of office automation, and, thus, have not changed their use of secretarial resources to ensure full benefit from the potential available.

Certainly, at this stage, the structure of management—junior, middle and senior—has remained unchanged and unaffected.

Post-Automated office jobs (late 1980's-early 1990's)

If the two previous stages can be described as the eras of computerisation and of word processing, then the period 5–10 years hence can be described as the era of the workstation and communications.

This period will see the greatest impact of office automation, and its effect will be felt across all sectors of the office worker population (and particularly in the management area).

The scenario we are portraying will be that of:

Individual workstations which could operate as data entry points, word processing workstations or administrative/managerial workstations covering records management, analysis, report production etc.

Department controllers, minicomputers, such as the DEC VAX computer, or the IBM System 36, which will provide communications facilities between all the workstations in an area or a department, enabling those workstations to have access to a wide range of relevant information files.

A host system – DEC's All-in-1, or IBM's DISOSS – which enables the department controllers to communicate with one another, perhaps in the same building, or perhaps across the world, thus ensuring that the documentation transfer is common, enabling a word processor to transfer a document to a minicomputer and for it to read the same on each machine.

This type of scenario is fundamentally different from that of, say, the early 1980s where the thought was that there would be one large machine – providing a whole host of facilities for all the intelligent terminals in a building. Instead, as described above, the difference is that the individual can manage his or her work procedures as he or she wishes. The individual is paramount over the big machine.

So how will this scenario affect the various clerical, secretarial and managerial jobs?

Clerical functions

The distinction between data preparation and data entry will be eliminated – all information will be input to the computer direct from original documents without any preparation in the interim. The 'paper factory' of the 1970s will be extinct – in its place will be rooms occupied by terminal operators controlling the input of material to the computer and the storage and retrieval of such information on computer filing systems.

Clerks as we know them will no longer exist – the individuals will be known as 'information processors'. Whether the clerks are taken over by the data entry operators, or the data entry operators are taken over by the clerks is irrelevant because the two jobs will be as relevant to the post automated office era as the Model T Ford is to the Ford Sierra.

The new role will be using user friendly interrogative software – a long way from the formal computer friendly software of the data entry operator. Similarly, the clerks will be expected to apply some appreciation of how the computer digests the entered information inputted rather than leaving that to the computer 'expects'.

What is particularly interesting is that the role of the 'information processor' need not be undertaken in a large office occupied by staff doing the same activity. Now, with the advent of communications, departmental information processing can be undertaken, thus allowing such processing to be carried out at the location best suited to it. So, for example, if insurance policies are sold by an insurance company's branch office, there is no need for that information to be sent to head office to be processed. An intelligent terminal based at the branch could enable the policy to be processed, and even produced at that location, thus cutting down the time spent before the potential customer becomes a satisfied customer.

Similarly, a salesman, out on his round of the territory, can take orders directly onto the portable computer he keeps in his car, and then, when he returns home each evening, connect his computer by telephone direct either to his office's mainframe or perhaps to a public electronic mail system, and the orders can be processed directly onto the computer.

Not only can the location of information processing be different from the large 'paper factories' of the past, but also the individuals concerned can be different. In the two examples given, the need for the traditional clerk/data entry operator has been eliminated, and the work has been done by someone for whom it is not the prime area of activity. Thus, the information processor of the future could be a secretary, or a manager, as well as being a traditional clerk.

How the information is processed depends upon the nature of the information and the speed of response required for it. Taking the latter, and the example of the salesman, the benefit of entering information by the sales-man may be only of significance if the customer delivery time is improved. If the deliveries are made daily, then obviously the direct entering is beneficial. However, if delivery times are monthly, or even longer, then it is better to leave the salesmen to do their job, and provide informa-tion processors to carry out the specific task of entering information.

Secretarial functions   Just as the traditional clerical role can be seen to diminish significantly, so, too, can we see the role of the secretary expanding significantly.

Of prime importance is the fact that the automated office for this period at least, will be based around keyboard tasks. Thus, those who dominate the keyboard arena of today will gain power and responsibility in the keyboard arena of tomorrow. The secretary is thus in a position of great opportunity to take advantage of the changes.

The introduction of electronic mail will aid the secretary in this role, alleviating a lot of the work associated with the typing of memos and internal reports (an IBM study showed that in large organisations, 90% of communications are of an internal nature). For instance, the need to photocopy reports and memos can be eliminated with electronic mail. Similarly, the problems of organising meetings of several people are minimised by being able to cross reference their diaries using the diary management part of the electronic mail system. By taking these tasks and reducing the time a secretary has to spend on them, the automated office will give the secretary more time to spend on other tasks. Fortunately, the opportunity to acquire skills necessary to deal with these other tasks will come along as part of the automated office. Software such as spreadsheet analysis and database management, combined with word processing report writing facilities will enable the secretary to undertake some of the less important tasks currently undertaken by management.

For example, with the information readily at hand, a secretary would be able to analyse and prepare a report on monthly sales figures (indicating such factors as customer mix, average price levels etc). In the past, such a task was regarded as a managerial responsibility, largely because it involved the collation of information, checking its validity, and interpreting the findings. Now most, if not all, of that can be produced easily on a personal computer, and the text added as appropriate.

The extent to which a secretary takes on managerial tasks depends upon two factors:

1   His or her abilities to do so.
2   The willingness of management to delegate some of those tasks.

Undoubtedly, modern 'secretarial' training courses are starting to recognise the need to develop the abilities to bridge the gap from secretarial to junior management. Equally undoubtedly, most of today's secretaries (an increasing percentage of whom are graduate trained) have both the desire and the personal attributes to make the bridge.

The management willingness is undoubtedly the difficult area, but we can assume that the pressures for management to acquiesce will be very great. Not least when they come to realise that the automated office provides the secretary with a career path which can be achieved – thus, those management that do not show the willingness will find themselves losing staff to those that do.

Hopefully, the change in responsibilities for the secretary will lead to a change in title – from one which is indicative of a job which has little career development, to one, such as Management Assistant, or Information Administrator, which can indicate another step in the career path, and not just the end of it altogether.

One of the results of such a change is likely to be more males entering the 'secretarial' role – not to be secretaries, but because they see it as part of the 'computer scene'. So female secretaries of today – take advantage now!

Unfortunately, this expansion of role for secretaries is unlikely to be seen for the typist. The ability of managers to be able to input text directly onto the screen will mean less opportunities for copy typing. Instead, the role of the typist – or word processor operator – will be to amend text entered initially by authors, and to undertake the generation of standard letters etc.

Whilst this role is unlikely ever to be eliminated, it seems clear that its importance, and the numbers involved will reduce as time goes on, and as managers and secretaries (or management assistants) use the automated office to its full potential.

Managerial functions

Currently, management do not fully realise the implications upon them of the automated office.

We have already described how management assistants will have at their disposal the tools necessary to undertake the work currently done by junior or middle management. The more the secretaries take on as part of their role, the less there will be for the junior and middle management levels.

Today, clerks and secretaries prepare and present information for the junior and middle managers to tabulate in various ways for subsequent presentation to senior management. We are now saying that in the future secretaries are in as good a position to tabulate the information as are their managers.

The outcome is almost inevitable. We will see a thinning in the ranks of junior and middle managers as they are superseded by management assistants taking on their responsibilities.

At the same time, the senior management will be able to query the computer directly to ascertain information they require without having to ask a subordinate to obtain the information. So the squeeze will come on junior and middle managers from the top down as well as bottom up.

How far these two grades of managers will be squeezed depends upon:

a   How wide the band is between junior and middle management – the wider it is, the more difficult to eliminate it, and the more difficult to determine the career path from management assistant to senior manager.

b   How specialist the management role is – if a technical qualification is required, then that too will make it difficult to eliminate the inbetween grades.

Those managers remaining in their posts will benefit from the easier acquisition of information and its manipulation – using database management and the spreadsheet analysis such as Lotus Symphony – and the ease with which they can communicate to their colleagues using electronic mail.

Undoubtedly, these facilities will make their existing job easier. Xerox undertook a study in the USA which showed that managers spend 25% of their time writing and 20% of their time doing clerical tasks – it is largely the latter area where managers will benefit. The extra time created should enable managers to explore areas for which they had little time. These new areas covered will give managers greater knowledge and control of the areas in their responsibility.

So within the space of 20 years, we are seeing the automated office having a significant effect upon the structure of the office, and the roles of people working within it. Deliberately we have stayed within the context of equipment as we know it today – largely keyboard-based – and software which is available today. Because of the way in which such equipment slowly penetrates the office marketplace, such equipment will have a strong presence until at least the early 1990s.

By that time, however, equipment such as voice recognition and software for artificial intelligence machinery will be available and beginning to be used in large numbers. The impact of such further changes will be studied in Chapter 6. Undoubtedly, the office of the year 2000 will look and function differently to that of 1990. For those individuals working in offices over that period, it will represent a time of great challenge and the individuals will need to demonstrate adaptability and flexibility.

Like all periods of change, they can occur haphazardly, without planning – in which case the after effects can be haphazard – or they can occur with some organisation and planning.

Our view is that compared to recent years, where the automated office affected specific or isolated parts of an organisation, the changes likely to occur over the next 5–10 years will pervade all parts of the organisation. As a consequence, there is too much at risk to treat it haphazardly. The next chapter deals with where organised planning is necessary and what the benefits are.

5 Organisation in an automated office

It could be said that, in the future, an electronic office without organisation will be like an unruly child. As stated at the end of Chapter 4, in recent years the need for organised, planned implementation was not significant. The consequences of such a deliberate lack of planning included the use of a variety of different manufacturers' machines within the same company or organisation, and different departments re-inventing the wheel each time they approached a piece of PC software for the first time.

However, the real automated office will require some strong guidance, direction and organisational planning to ensure real benefits are achieved and the implementation successful. A recent study by A T Kearney Ltd, a management consultancy, on behalf of The Department of Trade and Industry and the Institute of Administrative Management showed:

a Of those companies interviewed (235 in all), none had reached more than 80% of the benefits of IT, and most were around 50–60%.
b The consequences of the failure to align business and IT needs equates to nearly £1 billion per annum wasted.

Both this study in 1984 and one carried out in 1983 by the National Economic Development Office are worthwhile examining as to the successes and pitfalls of the automated office.

Each study is at different ends of the spectrum – the Kearney study being a personal interview and questionnaire responses on a large scale, the NEDO study being an in-depth analysis of 15 systems (which were known beforehand to have been implemented successfully).

The key points from the NEDO study* are that:

1 The individual management in charge of each project will almost certainly have been above average to achieve 15 successful implementations, and the emphasis on exploiting the system to achieve higher standards of performance may have been unusually great.

2 A number of line managers were very much involved in the design of the system – in most cases a 50/50 exercise between line management and DP professionals. This meant the line managers had to acquire considerable understanding of the technology as well as the ability to think in systems terms.

3 Most office workers found they shed routine work, spending more time on problem solving, redefining procedure to improve performance, or delivering a higher quality customer service.

4 Supervisors found themselves managing a work process rather than a group of people.

5 Whilst some skilled jobs were deskilled by the introduction of automation eg telephone engineers, draughtsmen, programmers, where these jobs were opened up by the automation to more junior staff, those staff had their skill levels enhanced.

6 Whilst the numbers of jobs remained the same in nearly all cases, because of jobs transfer within the organisations, there were job losses within the relevant section in 9 out of the 15 examples. Equally importantly, where jobs were created, they were almost all at graduate level.

The Kearney study† had similar findings, although the larger number of companies it covered made it inevitable that the problems of achieving a successful implementation of office automation would become readily apparent. The reasons it gave for success in office automation projects included:

---

* Quoted from an unpublished conference paper given by Carolyn Hayman of Korda Ltd. (A fuller description of the results can be found in '*The Impact of Advanced Information Systems: The Effect on Job Content and Job Boundaries*', available from NEDO.)

† Quoted from A T Kearney Limited, Management Consultants, '*The Barriers and Opportunities of Information Technology*'.

1   Quality of staff and their ability, cooperation between user and technical staff, training, and a clear definition of requirements.

2   A commitment towards the use of information technology – including an emphasis on the need to define IT objectives and therefore, the need to align IT needs with business needs.

The factors it described as 'barriers' to success included:

1   Management itself, ie a lack of appropriate cost/benefit analysis for justifying further investment, and a stated need to consolidate previous investments.

2   This barrier is lowest for those already advanced users, whilst those with little IT investment (and therefore most to gain) showed the most resistance. Thus, the important factor is to gain the interest and commitment of management to office automation.

Above all, the report criticised companies for not viewing office automation as part of their corporate strategies.

Having had the benefit of these two reports to highlight the need for organised planning, let us develop a blueprint for the factors that managers and secretaries involved in the implementation of the automated office should consider in their planning.

A planning blueprint

Office automation as a corporate strategy

Too often directors of a company are seeing office automation as an add-on to their company's activities, or alternatively merely a substitute for existing processes—for example, substituting a typewriter with a word processor, or a PABX telephone system with electronic mail.

What should concern the directors of such organisations is that while they may be relaxed in their attitude to the impact of office automation on their business, there are other parts of the world rushing into it headlong, and companies, including some in the United Kingdom, which are using it constructively to their corporate benefit.

For example, in the USA, it is anticipated that by 1987 there will be an equal number of electronic keyboards to the number of white collar workers. Similarly, the USA installed computer capacity in 1990 will be 1000 times that of 1970.

Growth of this magnitude cannot fail to affect the competitiveness of firms that take on office automation with a high degree of commitment. The benefits of such commitment are significant. The Kearney study shows that 'companies lagging in the use of information technology are six times more likely to have a poor financial performance, within their business sector, relative to the companies that lead in the use of information technology.'

With Britain employing 60% of its working population within the service sectors, and 30% of the total working population in office work, the effect of a committed approach towards office automation would be to offer the possibility of a significant boost towards individual company and the nation's international competitiveness.

In the USA, they have even tried to quantify the value of improved efficiency in office workers – 'Fortune' magazine quoted that if 50 minutes per day could be saved from each existing office worker's time, that would provide an extra $100 billion worth of worker time (or alternatively the same amount in an ability to make your products and services more effective and more appropriate to the end user).

Just as office automation can make your job more efficient, so, too, can it offer the opportunity to change the way you do it. One good example of this is one British building society that reviewed its approach toward office automation and information technology and came to appreciate that it offered a means of finding a highly competitive niche in the investment market. What it did was to offer its customers the facility of a Prestel based (viewdata) home banking service. This represents a valuable perk that can be offered to its customers, and, more importantly, attracts a particularly high grade customer—one who can afford a Prestel set. The building society also suffered from having relatively few branches, so with one sweep of the office automation technology, it was able to create an image of advanced technology, provide a substitute for its lack of branches, and appeal directly to people who are high investors.

Another example is the tour operator who provided a viewdata link to travel agencies, thus making that particular operator more attractive to sell because it was easier to book tours through them.

A last example of how office automation changes the way we do business is the automatic cash dispenser usually outside banks as a hole in the wall. Whatever the initial reason for their introduction, the benefits have helped the banks change their methods of operation. Until recently, the automatic cash dispenser allowed banks to close their doors on Saturdays, cope with bigger business levels with similar numbers of staff, and to reach out to their customers – as, for example, dispensers in factory workplaces or in department stores.

So it is clear from these examples, and the previous discussion on our businesses' competitiveness, that office automation cannot be hidden from view – it has to be in the forefront of any discussion on an organisation's future and it has to be treated as part of the strategic framework.

Office automation – who's responsible?

As a necessary follow-on from this last section, it ought to be clear to the reader that, with something so important, there ought to be one individual in the organisation who has a strategic responsibility for it.

In the 'era of computerisation' that we described in the last chapter, it was clearly within the area of the data processing manager's authority. This was sensible because the area of work was transferring from line managers responsible for clerks, to DP managers responsible for data preparation to a set format, and subsequent data entry. The work area of the DP manager could be totally isolated from the rest of the organisation – in fact in many organisations, the door into the DP department was always kept closed, and very few people entered the inner sanctum, *nor* were they encouraged to enter.

Now, as you will appreciate, when we consider the era of the workstation and communications, there are no closed doors, no barriers separating off parts of the organisation. Instead, office automation is becoming all pervading – we are almost at the stage where no office is sacred (undoubtedly there will remain the exceptions).

Thus the individual responsible for spearheading this change, and for recognising the commercial opportunities offered by the technology, must be someone who has a broad vision.

Ideally the individual should be a member of the Board – not necessarily the finance or marketing directors because they would have to impose their own discipline. Instead, there should be appointed either commercial technology directors, or it should be the managing directors themselves.

Please recognise that this role is not designed to have 100% control over office automation – we would expect to see the end user determining how they themselves use the technology – but it is intended to ensure:

1 The technology in use is compatible (both now and for the future).
2 There is support for the end user – perhaps in the form of information centres, where end users could obtain some practical applications support to get the most out of their equipment.
3 The initial implementations of the various pieces of equipment are carried out effectively, and the individuals concerned are kept updated of changes and trained accordingly.
4 The commercial opportunities of the technology are recognised and action taken to achieve their benefits.

Even with these responsibilities, the director concerned may not have (or need) authority over all the various activities – such as training, marketing direction or data processing management. What is essential is that these activities are tied together, and that the Board is aware of the needs of office automation to run effectively, and of the opportunities offered.

People – the implementation process

Once the senior management of an organisation have recognised the need to significantly raise the profile of office automation, the risk is that they stop at that point. They see office automation as a technology, rather than a change in the human process caused by technology introduction. It is a little like considering a car as an engineering advancement, without appreciating the need to train humans to operate it, and subsequently to appreciate the changes in society caused by human beings having cars which can transport them long distances at their will.

So when we talk of planning office automation, we must also talk of planning change in our office workers. What factors should we consider?

1   What are the objectives of the office automation implementation – what is it intended to achieve, and whom will it affect? If these are unclear in any respect, then there will be partial failure at least.

2   What are the pay-offs? We know (or we *should* know) what the management expect of the changes, but we need to ask ourselves – 'What are the benefits to our staff?' – because without being able to position such benefits, then the staff will be likely to resist change. One obvious benefit may be the ability to have a more responsible job. But if the member of staff is at the raw end – perhaps if their job is deskilled, and leaves them temporarily out of a job – how can we position the benefits? In this case, plan retraining, and make it clear from the outset that people in this position, will be offered retraining.

If the benefits are very insignificant to the individuals, then create another benefit – perhaps working more flexible hours – and relate the one to the other.

3   Who are the obstacles? Can the 'resistors' be identified beforehand? It may be an individual or it may be a group or a department. Perhaps the data entry department will be using new, more complicated equipment, or maybe it will be eliminated altogether because the data is inputted directly from the user departments. If examples such as these can be identified beforehand, then action can be devised to overcome any possible resistance, avoiding it altogether.

Equally, identify the 'cinderellas'. In other words, seek a group previously under-privileged, and whom other members of the organisation would regard as being lower in the pecking order. Then choose the 'cinderellas' to be your pilot group so that the other members of staff would be likely to say 'Well, if they have that piece of equipment, then clearly I deserve it, too.'

These factors are probably the critical ones to consider – and in communicating to staff before the implementation starts. So what are the actions we should plan as part of the implementation process:

1 Communicate your outline plans and objectives, so everyone knows what to expect.

2 When communicating, build in a sense of uncertainty about the change – get the staff to 'expect the unexpected'. We should not be seeking to cause concern about the uncertainty, but rather to force the staff to recognise that the technology is changing quickly and the future, unknown as it is, may be considerably different from the present.

3 Undertake pilots (use the 'cinderellas' in these where appropriate). The objectives of these pilots are, firstly, to tell the management the hidden problems; secondly, to tell the staff that the management have been anticipating the hidden problem; and, thirdly, to build a sense of desire on the part of the people not involved to become involved.

4 Tackle the 'resistors' with individual treatment, and, ideally, tackle them early on.

5 Involve the users in the design of the systems. This involvement could be either the manager (as in the NEDO study) or the operators (as in Enid Mumford's 'Designing Secretaries' 1983, and her work at ICI). In the case of the latter, the comment at the end of the study was:

'A spin-off effect of the study was the feeling that we now have a considerable amount of knowledge of word processing technology and the organisation, and we have become quite skilled at analysing problems and solutions.'

In other words, the involvement not just ensured the commitments of the individuals to the change, but caused them to think how they could improve their own effectiveness.

6 Recognise the need for strong training, not just for operators, but, as importantly, for the managers. Use the trainers as counsellors for the 'resistors'.

7 Continue the communication process throughout the implementation, so that staff are aware of changes, delays in schedule etc.

8 Ensure staff are aware of the benefits to them, and,

as part of the continuing communication, inform them of progress to targets, and achievements in areas that interest them – for example, 'flexible work is being used by all of XYZ departments because of the benefits of the new technology.'

Undoubtedly, there are other areas involved in the management of changes in which the reader is involved, or would wish to see included in this list. The objective of developing such an action plan is to ensure we recognise that an organisations's key asset for the future is its staff – such a plan helps to safeguard that asset in a sensitive manner and ensures we can achieve our business objectives at the same time.

People— training

We have included this aspect of planning as separate from the implementation process because we believe it should be recognised as one of the most important changes required. To date, training in the use of equipment for office workers by employers has been pitifully small. The last time most secretaries received any form of office practice training was when they left secretarial college.

This approach is dramatically different from the attitude of a manufacturing works manager if there was a similar investment in new technology. In this case, the factory workers involved would be trained in using the new technology – otherwise the works manager knows there is little likelihood of meeting the productivity targets. The same must be true for the office managers – who must recognise that in the future they must manage 'office productivity' just as their counterparts in manufacturing manage 'shopfloor productivity'.

The training necessary must not be of a 'one-off' nature.

Firstly, the equipment the office workers will be using is capable of being operated at different skill levels (see Manpower's categorising of skill levels – pages 42–3). Consequently, as each office worker gets used to operating the equipment at one level, the question of subsequent training arises to ensure the worker is able to use the equipment at subsequent skill levels in the most effective manner.

Secondly, each software manufacturer is constantly updating their packages – Lotus 1-2-3 has been updated to Lotus Symphony, WordStar to WordStar 2000, and the venerable IBM Displaywriter has had additional facilities, such as Chartpak, Reportpak and, more recently, the Personal Services facility. Even if the organisation decides not to update frequently, at some stage there will be a need to do so (perhaps to achieve other advantages or cost savings).

Thirdly, the machines themselves are updated. On average a piece of equipment is available on the market for 2–3 years before being superseded. Such changes may not be updated by the organisation at the earliest opportunity, but, speaking for Manpower's head office in the UK, we have moved through 4 different types of word processor, each one being an improvement.

Clearly, therefore, to benefit from the potential of office automation, and to cope with future changes, an organisation has to elevate training to a high priority position, and allocate resources commensurate with office automation's position in the organisation's strategies.

This does not require training to be an in-house, people intensive department. The speed of change means that the outside specialist training companies are more likely to be able to offer latest state of the art training, than an internal training department whose resources are being stretched keeping up with current needs.

The interfaces It became very clear in our chapters on machines and people that the automated office of the future would involve workstations – to give individuals the freedom to do their work in the most appropriate manner – and communications facilities to tie the individuals together in a cohesive whole.

Obviously, the former can only operate effectively if the latter has no obstacles. Hence, when planning an office automation programme, it is these interfaces that need to be understood, and catered for.

The type of interface that needs to be considered is:

1 Links between equipment If communication is to

work, then the equipment must be able to talk to each other, and also translate what each other is saying. A lot of work has been undertaken in this area – both technical work to ensure technical compatibility and legal work to ensure that manufacturers advise other manufacturers in sufficient time to enable the latter to follow new 'architectures'. In the case of technical work, there has been a legal case in the EEC against IBM, contesting that IBM gave insufficient warning to other computer manufacturers of its changes in machines and communications facilities. The case has been settled by IBM agreeing to give more notice of such changes.

Consequently, the problems for users of incompatibility have been alleviated to a greater extent, but it is nevertheless very important to check on the links between equipment.

2   Links between equipment and software   It is to this area that the problems of compatibility have transferred. The links can pose several difficulties.

Firstly, the communications software may be relevant for only certain pieces of equipment *and* for only certain types of software. Thus, for example, if a piece of text is transferred from one machine to another, each of which has different text-editing software, then the layout of the text may not be in the correct format for the receiving machine to word process.

Secondly, when software is introduced initially it is often available only for certain machines – for instance Lotus 1-2-3 and WordStar 2000 were designed initially for the IBM PC market. Thus, if a user buys software with the intention of using it throughout the organisation, there must be the machines capable of utilising it.

3   The links between office and non-office users   Often office automation is a misnomer, since the organisation may well automate non-office operations at the same time.

Examples could include the use of portable personal computers for use by salesmen, or even gas meter readers. Such additional aspects of automation need to fit into the total automation network – or have a buffer through which the information can be processed before entering into the main information network. Similar examples would include the use of bar code reading machines in shops and supermarkets.

The reason for highlighting non-office use is that there is little point implementing office automation for office use, only to find later that there are non-office uses for which the particular machines chosen intially may be incompatible (or more likely have cost inefficiencies when applied to non-office use).

The environment

So far in this chapter we have concentrated on the implementation process, the training needs of people, and the machines themselves. However, one of the most important factors to consider is the environment – which, if not considered in advance, can be as much a factor affecting the productivity of a system, as the people involved themselves. In addition, a poor environment can pose great problems for staff having to work within it and consequently affect the quality of their work (see the Appendix, Health and Safety in the Automated Office).

In 1983, ORBIT, a multi-client study* was published on the effects upon office design of information technology. The findings of this study caused considerable controversy, because it showed that information technology had a wide area of impact upon the office environment, and that the cost implications of ignoring this impact could be greater than the cost of the initial installation of office automation equipment:

1 Frequent downtime of equipment could be caused by uneven power supplies, static and dust, and cables being unmarked, causing accidental severing of them.
2 Buildings are often inadequate to meet the needs of the automated office. The costs of a building budget to ensure the equipment runs effectively could equal that of the equipment budget when it provides for raised floors, humidifiers, extra trunking etc.

* The ORBIT project produced by DEGW, architects; EOSYS, office systems consultants and Building Use Studies, design consultants, available from 8/9 Bulstrode Place, Marylebone Lane, London W1.

3 Staff operating the equipment suffered fatigue and discomfort from poor lighting, thermal control and unsuitable furniture.

4 The need to ensure flexibility in an organisation by moving people or reorganising departments to ensure it can comply with changes in technology, can be seriously restricted because buildings' systems have not been planned to accommodate change. Cables may not be easy to reroute, or lighting may be insufficient.

The environmental factors that need to be considered and planned in advance of the implementation of an automated office include:

1 Lighting VDU screens are reflective and people working at them will be affected by the lighting systems in the office – many of which create large amounts of glare.

Modern lighting systems can improve the lighting quality by reducing glare (and reducing running costs by 40% or more over older versions). These include uplighters, individual fluorescent task lights and overhead fluorescents with low brightness louvres.

2 Heat Whilst each individual piece of office equipment may not be high in heat emission, the concentration of them in particular areas can intensify heat emission in those areas, causing increased costs in air conditioning (which is normally intended to give an even temperature level) and increased staff discomfort.

Fig 6 demonstrates the heat emissions of various pieces of office equipment (see opposite).

Whilst these heat emissions are unavoidable if you are going to have office automation, there are actions you can take to minimise heat build-up:

- place machine intensive functions on the north side of a building (away from direct sunlight – in the northern hemisphere)
- place high heat emitters, such as photocopiers, in separate, well-ventilated areas
- turn off lights at midday

3 Noise With the exception of printers, automated

			WATTS
	1000	2000	3000	4000

Person — 100

Small micro — 60

Stand alone word processor (no printer) — 150

Desk top printer — 200

Multi function workstation including printer — 350

Line printer (ie large) — 800

PABX (120 extns) — 550

PABX (500 extns) — 4000

Floppy disk drive — 100

Display — 100

Large (67 Mb) disk drive — 1100

Desk top photocopier — 1000

Medium photocopier — 2200

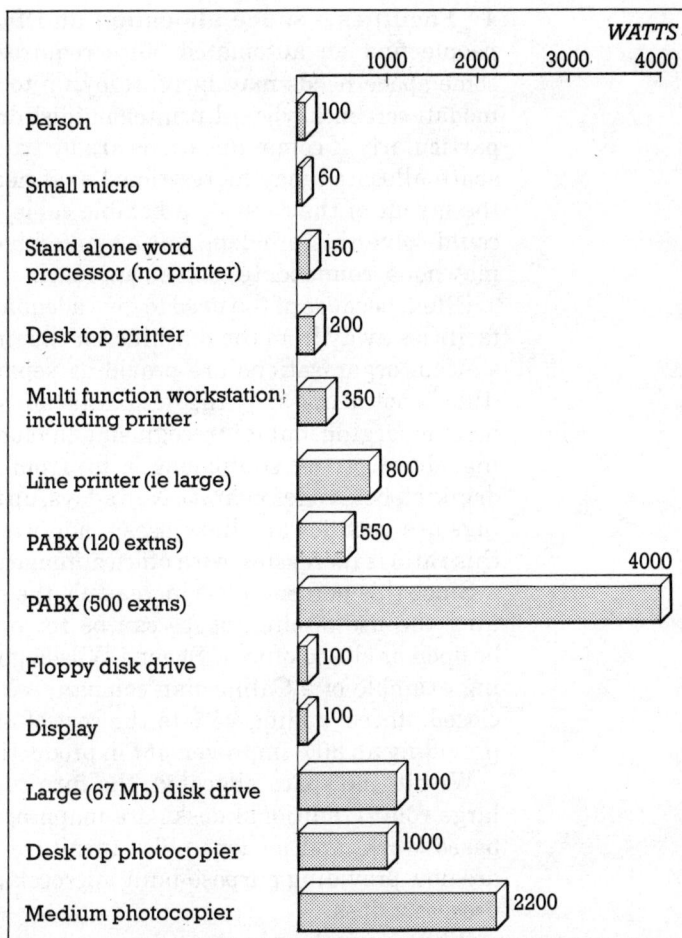

Fig 6   Typical heat emissions of equipment while running (on stand-by emissions are often substantial)

office equipment is generally not noisy, but this does not mean sound absorbent finishes, such as acoustic ceiling tiles and screens are not necessary. Often, in an open plan office, the use of such materials improves the ability of individuals to concentrate in adjacent work areas.

Printers, of course, should have either acoustic hoods, or some form of effective sound insulation screening.

4 Facilities – space allocation and furniture   Most people find an automated office requires more space – some space needs may increase by up to 50% to accommodate screen, keyboard, printer and disk drive. In addition particularly if communications are by trunked cable, the space allocated may be restricted as it needs to relate to the layout of the cables – a flexible cable routing system could solve this problem, but as stated before, buildings may not accommodate such an approach.

Often, because of the need to give adequate rest or break facilities away from the machines or the individual workstation, organisations are providing separate rest areas (this is not necessarily the humanitarian side of management emerging, but it is recognising that one way of avoiding abuse of the equipment is to avoid eating food or drinking beverages near it). Nowadays, up to 40% of buildings are used for ancillary uses – non workstations, and this ratio is increasing with office automation.

Since this percentage is increasing, the method of planning the use of office space can be reviewed – should it be open or closed offices? Sheena Wilson gave an interesting example of a Californian company which reverted to closed offices, adding 25% to the cost of office space, but providing an 80% improvement in productivity.

Within the space allocated, the furniture must play a large role. Traditional desks are inappropriate for VDU-based work, and modern office furniture manufacturers are now providing purpose-built microcomputer and word processor desks.

When we look at how managers sit when using a piece of equipment with a keyboard and a screen, we find they have a totally different posture to that of a secretary with a typewriter. The posture when using an electronic keyboard is very relaxed – like driving a car – and a secretary's chair is not only inappropriate, but in the long run, could cause physiological damage.

Within the areas of furniture, the question of power supplies has often been a low priority. Now, however, with IBM Colour PC using up to 5 sockets, the question of power supply planning is a vital prerequisite to ensure the automated office works at the turn of a switch.

We started this chapter with the words 'an electronic office without organisation will be like an unruly child'. We hope that in going through this planning blueprint, you will have come to understand those words, and to appreciate that the automated office must not be installed lightly without due consideration and also that the organisation and planning of the automated office must not stop once it has been installed. It must be continually reviewed to assess the impact of future changes. Chapter 6 will try to highlight some of these changes.

6   **A view into the future**

Writing this chapter we are reminded that in 1948, George Orwell wrote a book describing a possible scenario for 1984. Similarly in 1937, the League of Nations forecast future inventions and innovations – they neglected to include the atomic bomb and the jet aeroplane amongst other, now well-established, products.

Undoubtedly, most of what we describe here will happen. Unfortunately, it is what we do not describe here, including the invention that eventually will have a dramatic impact on society, that you need to look out for (if you can). Please treat this view as a view through a keyhole – your vision is restricted by the extent of the keyhole.

Let us separate our crystal ball gazing, by looking at the equipment – what it will be and what it will do; the office – what will it look like and what will it do; and the people – how they will work.

The equipment

The developments we can expect in equipment (hardware and software) are likely to fall into four broad categories:

- input/output developments
- artificial intelligence
- telecommunications
- miniaturisation

Input/output

The extension of the computer into telecommunications has meant that the manufacturers have been seeking new ways of utilising the benefits offered.

At the time of writing this book, the new personal computer, the 'One Per Desk' launched by ICL – supported by design advice from Clive Sinclair – demonstrates the easiest route to utilising telecommunications and that is by combining the computing facilities and the telephone facilities into one piece of equipment.

As a consequence of doing so, the machine offers the opportunity of using the PABX systems as a form of electronic mail, since each machine has its own modem included in it. Other manufacturers in the UK have this approach on their drawing boards now, and companies in the USA have already launched similar products.

However, this is not necessarily a full scale leap into new technology. IBM's use of digitised voice, planned to be available in 1985, could be regarded as more in this area. In this system, the computer can translate data and text into a digitised voice. Thus, a manager can be out of the office and ring up her workstation to check what electronic mail messages are waiting for her. The computer can 'read' the messages, translating them into digitised voice, and communicate them back to the manager.

The benefits of being in one's car, and yet at the same time being able to check your mailbox – at any time of the day or night – are yet to be assessed. The manager's assistant's function cannot be done away with by the addition of this facility – there will still be a need for them to prepare reports etc, and the benefit of not having to be on hand when the boss rings in is one of convenience and effectiveness rather than economy.

However, another voice development may offer these benefits in an economic sense. That development is voice recognition. In this facility, the computer can not only translate text and data into digitised voice, but more importantly translate voice input into data or text. Obviously, the problems of disentangling poor pronunciation, local dialects, or poor use of language are immense. Perhaps too immense. Nevertheless, the Japanese are thought to have cracked the problem and will introduce it with their fifth generation computers in the late 1980s.

It may be that voice recognition may initially cover only certain terms – perhaps for data entry use, terms like sales, customer numbers, sales value and quantity, as well as the digits. Even such limited recognition as this could have significant impact on the automated office. The need for keyboard skills and for the lower skilled jobs, could be reduced significantly, if not eliminated.

If the full development of voice recognition is quick enough, it may mean that managers will not have to be proficient in keyboard operation.

The addition of voice recognition combined with touch sensitive tools such as the 'mouse', or the 'touch screen', could allow managers to amend their own reports, insert text, and edit the report, without using a word processor operator. If we bear in mind that, ultimately, voice recognition could offer the ability to dictate directly to a computer, then we could see the word processor operator's role being diminished significantly.

Another development, whose introduction is likely to add more convenience rather than change the extent of the roles of the individual is image transmission, such as IBM's Scanmaster. Essentially, this links a facsimile machine to a computer. Facsimile transmitters have recently moved to a digital representation of the image – and obviously, this is ideal for input to a computer over an electronic mail circuit (an IBM senior executive showed a picture of a village which had been transmitted from England to the USA by satellite. The picture received on the computer screen was indistinguishable from the original photograph – except that in the lower right hand corner was a flashing white square which was the cursor).

The introduction of image transmission is likely to add more nails in the coffin of the photocopier (although obviously the latter will still be required for external communications).

Artificial intelligence

In the previous section we mentioned that the Japanese have been developing their fifth generation computers – the four generations are as follows:

1st generation 1940–52	– vacuum tubes
2nd generation 1952–64	– transistors
3rd generation 1964–71	– integrated circuits
4th generation 1971 and after	– LSI (large scale integrated circuits)

The Japanese are using this development in the manufacturing technology as a means of jumping over the Americans' heads. Whether the Americans will let them do so or not remains to be seen, but the telling point is that by 1990 we will be seeing the first of the computers with immense computing power and speed.

The introduction of such machines has alerted people to seek new and radically different applications for them. The most important of these is **artificial intelligence** (or expert systems). These are computer programs which have been written to replicate the human mind in thinking out questions relating to specialised subjects. The intention is that a human can pose the question, and the expert system can evaluate all the options and draw the right conclusion. A good example of such a problem is the procedures book for establishing whether or not someone is able to receive supplementary benefit and the amount they should receive (the written version is a book several hundred pages thick). It is possible to convert these procedures into an expert system, the counter clerk to input the relevant details for a claimant and the computer to work out applicability and amount.

Expert systems are already being developed – without waiting for the extra computing power. One such system has been developed by Rank Xerox in their UK personnel department. This system provides secretaries with the knowledge necessary to tackle personnel questions without having to refer upwards to their managers.

The introduction of a system such as this aids the erosion of the junior and middle management grades in an organisation, since not only do the secretaries have the information at their finger tips, they also have the expert system to provide the knowledge they are lacking. This erosion of management grades is capable of being associated with an added efficiency because each individual personnel problem is dealt with to the same standard of knowledge and procedure.

Expert systems, when combined with fifth generation computing power, will be able to 'learn' from the individual as they approach each problem. So when a person tackles a problem for the first time, the expert system will learn and understand that person's approach, and the second time he or she tackles a similar problem, the system will adapt to the individual's previous approach and offer a preferred and more efficient approach.

Undoubtedly, expert systems are the next era of computers. Their impact may be limitless, and they can bring the benefits of computerisation to a far wider range of the population than ever before.

Telecommunications

The benefits of telecommunications have been introduced largely to improve the facilities offered by computers. However, we should expect that there will be additional improvements in the telecommunications facilities themselves.

For example, the phone-in-the-car which until now has been the luxury of the managing director, will become an every day necessity, just as most cars now have a radio. The portable phone need not stay only in the car – ultimately, with increased miniaturisation, the personal phone carried on the individual will become the norm.

Clearly, one of the benefits of having the carphone is that now portable computers, combined with the carphone, can make use of the electronic mail facility from anywhere – an office will not be required.

Similarly, the modern telephones have been able to offer three way audio conferencing. In the future, more use will be made of video conferencing as a means of having important discussions. Currently, the obstacles have been the need to use studios or set up offices to ensure the individuals are positioned correctly for the cameras. However, just as phones are being built into the personal computer workstation, so too could a miniaturised camera, with the individual using the VDU screen (split, say, into four windows) to view the other participants in the discussion.

Miniaturisation

What must be recognised is that there are opportunities for miniaturisation still to be achieved. If you were to look inside the workings of a personal computer, you would be surprised at how much empty space there is. In fact, the personal computer could be reduced further in size, if the screen could be made smaller (and the tube less large), the keyboard less mechanical, and the disk drive less bulky. Yet, some of these are possible. The tube, which is the dictating factor when it comes to the screen, has already been 'flattened' by Clive Sinclair, making it less bulky, and capable of fitting into a large envelope. The keyboard size is determined by ergonomics, but the addition of voice recognition, the mouse and icons, could change all that. The disk drives are already changing, because of the availability of dual and treble density disks, and the introduction of the Sony standard smaller disks.

Even now a new personal computer has been designed for the British Government's civil servants, that can be fitted into a small briefcase, enabling the civil servant to work at home – or in the train, whilst leaving room for the sandwiches! Miniaturisation will have its biggest effect on how the office is organised, and how much room is required for the equipment.

The office

The four areas just discussed are the impact areas for the equipment – but how will future changes such as these (as well as existing changes not fully implemented) affect the offices of the future?

There are probably two main aspects we need to consider – the location of offices and the nature of offices.

Location of offices

During the 1970s, there was a move on the part of large companies to move their head offices out of high rent and rates areas such as Central London, and in to lower cost suburbia and provincial cities.

These moves, whilst saving on occupation costs, often resulted in other costs increasing – particularly since senior management had to spend much of their time travelling to and holding meetings in London.

Now office automation offers the opportunity to correct these adverse cost factors and to add to the benefits of moving out of major cities. Often the benefits of locating a head office in a major city include:

- ease of communication with customers
- ease of getting people together for meetings in a central location

- ease of recruiting the right people for that head office

Office automation will not completely overcome these three factors, but it will reduce their importance to a considerable extent.

For example, communications with both customers and colleagues fall into two basic categories: the provision of information and the making of decisions. It is the former which is eased by automation, since the information required can be more easily acquired and more easily shared between interested parties (inside and out).

Our experience of meetings is that firstly, much time is spent discussing what information is required (that can be carried out under office automation either by electronic mail, or by audio conferencing, where all parties are linked by telephone or, in the future, by video conferencing where all parties are visible to each other). There is, thus, not the necessity to get together in one office building to discuss information needs.

Secondly, our experience is that having decided what information is required, the meeting usually adjourns for one or two weeks, whilst someone obtains that information. That adjournment can be shortened, if not eliminated, by everyone involved in the discussion having access to a terminal, and one of the discussion parties interrogating the data available, the results of that interrogation being shown on all parties' screens. The third stage of any meeting is the decision making based on the information available, and whether or not the individuals need to meet together depends upon the nature of the decisions and their implications.

Thus, what this previous description identified is that meetings can become easier under the aegis of office automation. No longer will it be necessary all the time for individuals from all parts of the country to meet physically in the same place. This applies both to internal meetings and external meetings, particularly those whose sole purpose is the imparting of information such as supply requirements etc.

It is considerations such as these which have made many large companies think of moving their offices out of major cities. One company, Rank Xerox, is already in the process of moving out of Central London to Marlow, about 30 miles away. It has been able to do so because of the reduced need for face-to-face communications as a result of Xerox's high use of office automation equipment. This has enabled them to take advantage of the high savings available in occupancy costs. At the same time, their prior use of office automation equipment provided the communications systems necessary to enable them to transfer many of their workers and managers from being permanent employees to being part of their networked 'outworkers'. This transfer of employment status meant a reduced headcount in their head offices which further allowed the opportunity to move offices.

The nature of offices

Undoubtedly, as this last comment would suggest, in the future, not only will we see new provincial locations for offices, but also a different nature of office. Clearly, it is likely that the changing nature of employment will cause the size of the office to be reduced – this is because of employment changes and not necessarily because of automation – studies so far show that few, if any, jobs are lost because of automation.

So how will a typical office change over the next few years:

1 Obviously miniaturisation will affect the share of office space devoted to equipment.

The area of space occupied by computers has diminished, so that today, departments are using a dedicated department mini to run their own systems. Even that mini will diminish in size and cost so that we will see the 'mini' moving from filing cabinet size to enable it to be located under an individual's desk.

Perhaps the biggest space and cost saving from miniaturisation will not come from reductions in computer hardware (after all, they are really pretty small already), but from reductions in telecommunications equipment sizes. Previously, the main physical disadvantage of local area networks was laying cables all around the offices. Now, however, there is an invention – NectarRing – which avoids all the additional cabling and instead enables you to plug into your nearest power socket and instantly communicate with your colleagues in adjacent offices. How successful this will be depends upon many factors, but it is a clear sign of the way things are moving.

We should recognise, however, that we are not only talking about the overall size of the office. The size requirement for an individual's office will change. Even today, portable telephones (which previously were for the millionaire set) are coming into our offices. That change in itself should make desk space more usable rather than committed to phones.

Another aspect is the size of the personal computer, as used by managers. What is emerging, in addition to the IBM PC configuration, is the lap-size portable personal computer – such as that introduced by Epson. It is clear that not all managers want the bulk of an IBM PC sitting on their desks, or in their offices, using up much valuable space. Instead, they will move to the lap-size portables, perhaps with only a limited screen facility and then whenever they need the bigger versions, plug the lap-size into them, and work from the bigger screen and memory base.

2   In the previous section we discussed miniaturisation, but that assumes existing technologies meet all our requirements and that there will be no further developments.

That clearly is not so, and what we are beginning to see is the convergence of existing, but parallel running technologies.

An example just beginning to take form is the laser video disk, combining with the microcomputer in an interactive sense. The laser disk is the successor to the video tape, whose characteristics mean that, unlike the tape, any piece of required image memory can be accessed instantaneously rather than by running through the tape. This facility is just beginning to benefit the training (and sales promotions) department where individuals can be trained (or sold to) using a combination of micro and laser video.

This exciting possibility is now being extended to filing of complete facsimiles of printed documents. This system, Megadoc, introduced by Philips, stands a very good chance of realising the claim of the paperless office – at least as far as the filing cabinet is concerned. This system has already been used by the publishers of *Stern* and *Die Zeit* to store 4 million press cuttings for fast electronic retrieval by journalists. Currently, this system is too expensive for everyday office use, but undoubtedly within 10 years, systems such as this will become commonplace and enable not only quick and easy access to the printed document, but also dramatic reductions in the space occupied by the traditional filing cabinet (or the company's reference library).

3   Obviously, if these first two factors were the only ones, then we would see significant reductions in office sizes over the next 10 years. However, a counteracting factor is likely to be the recognition by designers that offices where occupants are working at screens regularly can be dull, uninteresting and unsocial places. The need for the VDU operators to spend only short times at their screens to avoid eye strain, backache and fatigue, mean that the offices currently being designed include larger rest areas whose purposes are:

a   To provide a rest area encouraging people to take breaks, so as to reduce the effect of stress and fatigue from screen operation.

b   To provide a stimulating area where social interaction can occur – the result being, hopefully, a better motivated staff.

These areas are not only larger than currently, they are also deliberately better designed to encourage use of social time by the employees.

The people   As we can see, there is a recognition that people's needs and abilities will be changing in offices of the future, but what will be the role of people in the future office – what will they be doing, and where will they be working?

What will they   It is pretty clear that some of the equipment developments
be doing?   discussed earlier in this chapter are going to have a significant effect on the nature of people's work.

Voice recognition will have significant (and possibly disastrous) effects on the clerical and junior secretarial skills.

In effect, it could possibly mean that a manager, instead of dictating to a secretary (either directly as shorthand, or indirectly via an audio tape) could dictate directly to a machine and have the words appear on the screen, to be immediately edited prior to transmission. This equipment development could, thus, significantly reduce the need for correspondence secretaries.

On the other hand, artificial intelligence, or expert systems, could have the opposite effect for the manager's assistant. This development will give junior staff the ability to make professional or managerial decisions by using the knowledge and advice displayed on the screen in front of them. The consequence of this change is likely to be for the managers' assistants to have an even more prominent role, since there is the possibility of their genuinely taking over the middle management role by acquiring from the computer the information normally only available to an experienced middle manager.

Those readers who are students should rest assured – both these developments will only start to play their full role from the 1990s onwards, and even then only in the bigger organisations. Nevertheless, we all need to consider the implications of changes such as these, both for our own concern and for that of organisations.

This discussion has concentrated so far on the effects on junior staff in an organisation. Equally as interesting when it comes to a 5–10 year view is what the middle and senior staff will be doing.

Our views in this respect are greatly affected by our understanding of the employment market and how that will change in the same time scale. The clear indication is that there will be an increased tendency towards use of contract specialised outside resources – these resources could range from accounting personnel (as is commonly the case nowadays) to marketing personnel and 'personnel' personnel.

The typical organisation in the 1990s is likely to represent a core of permanent individuals whose abilities or tasks are highly pertinent to the organisation, and who utilise the resources of outside organisations. This core of personnel in an office could easily be the senior management team supported by managers' assistants and junior managers using expert systems and advanced computerised telecommunications to manage the operational needs of the organisation. Undoubtedly, there will be other core staff, dependent upon whether the organisation is manufacturing or service orientated, private or public. Nevertheless, this slim 'superstructure' is likely to be accepted as the norm in the 1990s.

Already some organisations have made steps in this direction. Rank Xerox with their networking 'Xanadu' project is a highly successful example. Based on their experience, there seem to be some interesting implications for the people based in the core:

a Even though outside contractors may have been previously employed by the organisation, as is the case with Ranx Xerox, the use of such contractors places an added responsibility on the core personnel remaining – they have to start buying the services of individuals whose work they previously managed. This forces them to be far more critical of the work demanded of the contractors. It also makes them more diligent when requesting, for example, extra information – now they have to evaluate whether the information they receive justifies the extra cost of obtaining it by requesting a contractor to do the work.

b The manager's assistant, as the person normally coordinating the contractors, becomes a key individual in that organisation. Now that assistant probably comes to know more about what is going on than the manager himself. This knowledge base could represent a serious loss if the individual were to leave the organisation for any reason. Due to this, it is clear that management will require computerised systems to provide them with status reports on the contractors to avoid such an event. This should not be a problem since much of the communications with the contractors will be by computer links – even the single individual business will have their personal computer in their office to do their own work on, as well as communicate with customers.

The result of this slim superstructure will be a group of

generalists, whose roles are to gather information, from which to make strategic decisions, supported by a team of managers' assistants. These managers will be heavily equipped with office automation, giving them the abilities to make significant decisions (expert systems), and the responsibilities of managing and communicating with the many specialists whose skills are contracted into the organisation as and when required.

Where will they be working?

The type of organisation structure outlined above highlights that the location of the workers will itself be changing, and, in this respect, we are not talking about whether the office is located in central London or the suburbs, but, instead, where the office worker does his or her work.

If we look, firstly, at that group of core personnel, it seems likely that office automation will enable their working life to be more flexible. Obviously, a lot of their time will be spent in their office, for meetings and such like, but equally obviously, the telecommunications will enable them to work at home and receive all their calls diverted via their office workstation or office telephone. The extent to which they spend their time in the office, or at home depends upon:

a   The frequency the office has meetings or personal visitors.
b   Their need for social inter-action.
c   The philosophy of the organisation and the nature of the product that it provides.

A similar scenario becomes apparent with the outworker or contractor. That individual could work at home communicating with customers and suppliers by electronic mail, or, as an alternative, could band together with other outworkers to form an 'office-shop' at which all the services they require are provided at a cost considerably less than if they operated as individual offices. Such 'office-shops' are already being considered now, and the type of services provided include joint use of secretaries, mini or mainframe computers and telecommunications facilities. One important reason for many outworkers joining together in this form of communal activity is social inter-action.

Nearly all such individuals came from larger organisations, and find working on their own, at home, can be demotivating, providing little interest with their working life.

The one thing that is clear is that by the 1990s there will be a lot of office work being done partly at home – either by outworkers or by permanent core personnel. One attraction is the increased flexibility home working can give – flexitime can now cover all hours of the day and night, instead of just 8 am – 8 pm. Another attraction is that people seem to see a benefit from having a portable computer available at home – perhaps the reason is they can do some of their own domestic activities on it.

Conclusion As a conclusion let us try to highlight some of the areas that will be different, say, in 1992 compared with 1985:

1   There will be a proliferation of electronic keyboards – about one for each white collar worker in the UK. This means an extension of office automation in all sizes of business.
2   The use of office automation equipment will be simpler and more user orientated – developments such as voice recognition and expert systems can only achieve success if they are just this.
3   Communication by electronic mail and other computerised telecommunications will become faster and easier, changing the pace of business, and quickening decision making.
4   Large organisations will recognise fully the implications of office automation and begin to structure their offices and personnel to take best advantage of office automation.
5   As a result, we can see a thinning out of junior and middle management ranks, these individuals being superseded by well educated management assistants.
6   More specialist functions will be contracted out – the management of them being aided by computerised telecommunications.

As stated at the beginning of this chapter, it is relatively easy to look at current state of the art and extrapolate

5–10 years hence and talk about how such development will affect the future. However, it could well be that it is what we do not see now that will have the biggest effects.

In the next chapter we revert to the present and highlight some tips for the successful implementation of the automated office.

7 **The successful automated office**

So far we have been discussing developments in office automation – how it affects people, organisations and equipment – and looking forward to where we might be going over the next 5–10 years. Now, however, is the time to look at what we can do to make office automation more beneficial to us – both us as individuals and as organisations. A constant reminder should be *'machines are made for men, and not men for machines'*.

In this chapter we will look at office automation from two points of view – the manager's viewpoint, representing the organisation and the secretary's viewpoint, representing the individuals in an organisation – highlighting the basic questions to be considered at the time of the introduction of office automation.

The manager's viewpoint

The manager, when faced with office automation is not just faced with the acquisition of a new typewriter (as may have been the case in the past) but should recognise that not only could the total investment (people and equipment) run into 6 figures, but also that it could, *and* should, have a dramatic impact on the competitiveness of the organisation. In that respect, the manager should appreciate that prior planning of an office automation strategy is essential – the following are the types of questions which he or she should ask beforehand:

1 Why am I considering office automation? Unless the manager understands why the organisation wants to introduce office automation, it will be doomed to failure. Whilst the resources may be there, the commitment to make it happen will not be available because of a lack of understanding of what the purpose is. In this respect, it is essential that the manager relates office automation project back to the organisation's strategies. Is the project designed to cut costs, add quality to the product or service, add a 'product' differentiation for the organisation, or enhance the level of decision making? These questions must be answered beforehand, and with them there must be an appreciation that office automation does not only affect office work but should be seen in the whole context of how the organisation carries out its business.

If this awareness and understanding occurs, then it can help the organisation to utilise its automation investment in areas it had not previously anticipated – those areas adding to the competitiveness or the effectiveness of the organisation concerned. We have already discussed the impact of office automation on such organisations as the Nottingham Building Society and the tour operators. In each instance, the organisation thought laterally and recognised that office automation would give a competitive advantage larger than merely through cutting costs.

Other organisations could have similar opportunities provided they have the commitment to take advantage of them.

2   Who is responsible for office automation?   One of the biggest dangers today is for organisations to allow their office automation system to grow unchecked. Whilst it may be desirable to let each individual have control over their use of their workstation, this can be carried too far, including the choice of equipment and software. Inevitably, the problems of compatibility, communications, and access to common information bases need to be settled before commencing – not after. Similarly, without the identification of a single individual responsible for the development, spin-offs which may improve the organisation's effectiveness (as discussed earlier) may not be spotted – and even if they are, may not be implemented properly.

The question arises which individual should have the responsibility. It is important that there should be a board director who has total responsibility for office automation. Without such high level commitment the project could

be less of a success. Ideally, the director should be able
to identify commercial opportunities – in this respect, it
is not necessarily the traditional finance director who
should have the responsibility. Instead, the managing director or a commercial director should have this authority,
and should recognise they are not merely buying typewriters but are structuring their organisation's future.

3 Planning for the future? What should be clear by
now is that office automation will affect the way in which
the organisation does business *in the future*. Consequently, although it is essential that plans are laid to reflect existing situations, there must be some forethought
as to how the organisations's structure will change over
time, and there must be an in built flexibility for the system. This flexibility may be needed either for changes
within the existing structure, or to accommodate developments outside this structure. It may sound like crystal
ball gazing, but even the minimum of forethought will
pay off.

4 Pilots? One of the biggest mistakes for office automation projects can be assuming things really are as they
appear in the formal office structure. Instead, when you
look deeper into the workings of an office, informal communications become apparent which tend to short-cut the
formal systems. When office automation is applied it can
reflect a formal procedures system which is already inef-
fective also.

There are two actions which should be carried out to
avoid these costly errors:

a Make certain the procedures are rationalised before
you start automating them.
b Carry out pilots to ensure the systems pick up all the
benefits of the short-cuts in the informal system.

These pilots serve another purpose, in addition to that
of improving the formal and informal procedure. That purpose is to ensure all the individuals concerned are committed to the introduction and believe that their comments
have been listened to.

5 Involve the staff? What has been clear from those

office automation projects which have been investigated is that the really successful ones are those which:

a   Ensure the line management participate with the DP management in the development of the systems.

b   Ensure that all the staff are made fully aware of the changes planned, and that they believe them to be beneficial to them. Thus, even where the new systems may result in staff being under more strain or pressure, such as those involved in long periods in front of a VDU, then those staff should be provided with other benefits either directly, such as a changed working routine, or indirectly or even created – for example a pleasant rest room or free coffee. The offering of these staff benefits should be emphasised so as to be clearly seen to relate to the benefits gained by the organisation through the introduction of office automation.

There are two other considerations involved when it comes to managing the implementation involving the staff:

a   For those members of staff expected to be against the developments, use some means to overcome their objections. For example, either let them be the subject of the first pilot to make them feel special, or if they are normally felt to be superior, then deliberately delay their involvement by choosing a less preferred group, thus causing those against it to ask to be involved. Whichever route is tackled it is essential that these staff members should be identified and tackled to ensure the project's success.

b   Since the first office automation project will cause unforeseen structural changes, and without doubt will be followed by a second project later on, it is essential to make the staff aware of this. In this respect it is necessary to foster an *expectation of the unexpected*.

6   Training?   Probably one of the most important considerations after the choice of hardware and software is that of training, and yet most organisations seem reluctant to give it great thought.

The reasons for this are twofold:

a   The staff they will be training include secretarial and clerical, and, in the main, these staff have not normally been the recipients of organisation provided traning.

b The cost of the training now represents a much larger proportion of the hardware cost (now much reduced) compared to, say, 10 years ago when the hardware for a comparable performance might have cost 100 times as much. Consequently, the management ask the question – 'Do I need to pay for training for staff to use a piece of equipment costing only £5000?'

The responses to both these arguments are, of course, 'yes'. The key to successful utilisation of the potential offered by an office automation system lies in the users understanding fully what it can offer and how they can achieve it. This training covers not only the regular users – the secretaries and junior managers – but also the irregular users (most of whom if not properly trained would waste far too much time on the machines) as well as the authors of documents who, if they understand the system, can make the production of such documents simpler for all concerned! Training must raise itself in the priorities of an organisation, at least as far as office automation is concerned, and should be regarded as a programme that continues after the initial implementation has been completed.

7 Does the environment matter? As discussed in an earlier chapter, it is essential we tie environmental changes in the office into an office automation strategy. It is fairly pointless saving costs through office automation if we're dissipating them at the same time by additional costs as a result of over-heating, costly cable runs, or, most importantly, higher staff turnover demotivation as a result of badly planned (noisy and over-heated) offices.

The costs involved in any office automation strategy are high – it is senseless not to consider all aspects of the effects of office automation at the same time as introducing new equipment. Just as we should consider all aspects of data processing, text processing, telecommunications and office services within our strategy, so too, should we consider the improvement of the environment.

8 Monitor performance? Just as with a major manufacturing capital investment, we should plan beforehand to monitor performance, not just of the machines but, more importantly, how people use the machines. This monitoring (or advisory) programme should be a continuous programme, not terminating once the project is up and running, enabling the organisation to cater for staff changes, workload and software changes.

The secretary's viewpoint

Inevitably some of the questions a manager should ask before undertaking office automation are the same as a secretary would ask, or any other individual in the organisation, although from a different perspective. For the sake of completeness, we shall include them in the total set of questions listed here:

1 The choice of equipment for you? Whilst it may be impossible (and you may not have the necessary skills) to decide what is the right equipment for you, you should ensure you play a significant role in specifying your needs from which your equipment is chosen. For instance, the organisation may have chosen to buy IBM throughout – a decision to which you could not have contributed – but, within that overall decision, there are a variety of machines available offering a whole host of alternative use facilities. If you do not specify your needs, then you may find your work constrained, and, more importantly, you may find yourself unable to expand your responsibilities to wider areas. In this respect, you should ensure that your needs specification includes a view of the future – and this is mostly appropriately done with your boss, identifying what additional or wider responsibilities you may be able to take on in the light of office automation.

2 Get involved in office automation development? A follow on from the previous point, it is clear that those individuals involved in these developments will be able to create their opportunities for the future – whether it be through understanding the machines in a technical sense or through understanding how applications can be better developed.

To achieve this involvement (and ultimately career opportunities) you need to spend time understanding all aspects of the equipment they have, and keeping up to date with developments in office automation generally.

Experience so far of office automation has shown that individuals can advance themselves based on their office automation experience, regardless of where they started in an organistion – and where they might have ended up if their career had been based on their original skills.

3 Training? As a consequence of this last point, it is essential that the secretary insists on all the training necessary – and again, not just to cover the basics, but advanced skills training and training in new developments as they arise. From your point of view, this type of training is not merely vocational, in a market as young and fast developing as office automation it is more like obtaining professional qualifications.

There is another point, and that is, of course, by understanding the machines better and hence making your work easier, you will find more job satisfaction – probably more important in the initial stages than career opportunities.

Of course, to gain the greatest benefit from training, it is necessary for your colleagues – more importantly, your boss – to have a similar level of training, or of appreciation of office automation. You should bear in mind that most senior people may be wary of new technology – do not thrust your new found skills at them but encourage them as a partner to understand and consequently gain the best out of the new technology.

4 Careers? The time of introduction of office automation is the time to broach the subject of career development. Your superiors should have given some thought to this, and even identifying whether or not this has happened will help clarify for you how successful the organisations's office automation developments will be.

If you are able to prompt the thought that people are interested not just in how office automation will affect their job now, but in how career opportunities will change in the future, then it will be of benefit to you, your colleagues and the organisation itself.

5 Can you take advantage of office automation in your work? Even when you have had all the training, and understand how to utilise office automation to the fullest, you may be restricted.

To ensure you able to do so, you need to:

a Change the way in which you do your work to reflect the abilities of the system. This may mean simply (although sometimes laboriously) changing the layout of standard documents to accommodate a procedure already available in the machine. Alternatively, it may mean a total rethink of one area of your activities to ensure you can spend your time more effectively.

b Discuss with your boss some areas of your responsibilities (and those of your boss) including the authority that goes with those responsibilities. A good example is where a boss regularly produces a report including, say, an analysis of sales turnover. In the past the boss may have regarded that analysis as within his own area of responsibility – now, however, the secretary could undertake that analysis and prepare the report, in one activity, using the workstation both as a word processor and as a spreadsheet analyser. The report could be presented to the boss for a sign-off. Both parties would need to recognise that their areas of responsibilities have changed – and, if the sales turnover (or more likely salary information) is regarded as confidential, then so too have the authority levels.

This is an example of how the secretary's job becomes the manager's assistant, but the way in which it happens is by both parties discussing and agreeing the changes.

6 A comfortable and safe environment? You may be one of the individuals likely to spend most of your time in front of a screen, and as such are in the best position to identify possible areas of concern in the office environment as it stands now. Again, like careers, it is less use discussing the subject of the environment once the office automation development is up and running – for a start, there may not be the budget available at that stage. The type of areas you need to bring up as queries for the attention of the individuals responsible include:

a Will the lighting be satisfactory? Will it cause glare? Will the positioning of the workstations close to windows cause dazzle on the screens?

b Is the right seating available – or will it be made available? There is a difference between the type of chair necessary for typing at a typewriter and one for typing at a keyboard and screen – and that difference could cause backache if not handled properly.

c Will the noise of printers be baffled? Undue noise would cause lack of concentration as well as dissatisfaction at working in that office.

d Will there be adequate heating control, including air conditioning to counter heat emissions from the equipment involved?

As a last point, dealing with safety, rather than comfort, you should discuss what are the ideal length of periods for working at a workstation. Most organisations should have a view on this question. It is important not just from an eye safety angle, but also because the organisation should recognise that there are times when breaks from this activity are beneficial and possibly, essential.

Another safety factor, which is probably less important now is radiation emission from VDU screens – most manufacturers seem to be aware of this concern and have taken steps to reduce it to an acceptable level.

7 Communications – informally? Most bosses find that their secretaries are the best information source they have, telling them of significant changes even before they know of them. The bosses need to appreciate that there may be less oportunity for such informal communication in the automated office. Consequently, the provision of a communal area is not only a benefit as a break from working at a workstation, it could also be a significant factor in maintaining the informal communications system. The reader should not confuse this communication with gossip – often a secretary can advise the boss of forthcoming changes which can ensure the boss sets the right priorities in advance of fully knowing about them.

8 What is the objective of the system? You, as an individual need to be aware of what the organisation's initial objectives for the system are. After all, you will be one of the people involved in making these objectives happen.

Any good organisation will involve the staff at the outset and explain the objectives. If this is not the case, it should do so. A better understanding on your part of what these objectives are and how you can help achieve them will mean greater personal satisfaction. It will also help you see a larger picture of where the organisation is going and what part you may play in that direction.

9 How will the performance be monitored? From your point of view it is important to understand whether the performance of the system will be evaluated and if so, how? As well as being able to establish whether what you are doing is in line with this evaluation, you will also be able to contribute to whether or not the evaluation is appropriate to your area.

Clearly, if the criteria relates to something as simple as letters typed per hour, and you have been able to expand your role to take on statistical analysis which your boss did previously, then the evaluation criteria could be inappropriate for you and colleagues in your position.

This chapter has set out to highlight a number of basic questions which must be considered by individuals and organisations at the time of introduction of office automation. The more detailed the reader wishes to go, the more numerous and the more detailed the questions can become. Nevertheless, above all, there are three basic rules that an organisation should address before office automation commences:

1 Look to the organisations's needs and strategies – any office automation project must support them and help to develop them.

2 Look to the organisation's staff – the staff must be made aware of the reasons for the projects and must be given the facilities (training, authority and equipment) to utilise the potential to the full extent.

3 Look to the future – office automation is not a once and for all project – it enables organisations to handle future needs, and most importantly to control and direct its own future. The organisation's executives must recognise this and be committed to it. Only then will they be able to take full advantage of office automation.

With these thoughts in mind, we wish you *bon voyage* on your voyage of discovery in the world of office automation.

Appendix Health and safety in the automated office

There has been much argument over recent years as to the extent to which the new technology office equipment is hazardous. It seems clear that all parties to the argument agree that hazards do exist. On that basis, and rather than getting into arguments over whether the hazards are serious or not, here are some suggestions for actions to minimise them:

1 Health – physical problems: (eyestrain, backache, over-heating and low humidity problems) The suggested solutions include regular breaks from the screen. Where negotiated by trade unions, these breaks vary eg The Post Office agreement specifies 100 minutes maximum per day in front of a screen with a maximum of 50 minutes without a proper break; the Banking Union, BIFU, recommends 4 hours maximum operation per day, and the TUC, a 20 minute break for every two hours operation. In addition, the screens should be maintained regularly to avoid blurring of the display, or screen flicker, and the lighting should be designed to avoid glare.

As regards posture complaints, the use of a proper chair is one solution. In addition, however, the operator needs to be trained to sit properly, and also to position the screen and keyboard on the desktop correctly.

Overheating and humidity complaints emanate from the same source – the inadequacy of buildings in handling the automated office equipment. As well as providing the right air conditioning and humidifiers, the provider of these systems should ensure that there is localised control. Often, these problems are psychological as much as physical, and by providing the ability for an individual to control their own environment, these problems can be considerably lessened.

2 Health–psychological problems Although largely unresearched as yet, we ought to recognise that unless office space is planned carefully with staff in mind, there will undoubtedly be problems for staff sitting in cubicles facing a screen all day. The extent to which this is a problem depends upon the nature of the job, and the word processor operator, typing copy all day long may suffer the worst. Action needs to be taken to avoid boredom and loss of job interest. We also need to recognise that many people come to the office, not for the work, but for the community. Our rest areas should not be white walls with uncomfortable seating – we ought to ensure they are places where a community can develop.

3 Safety There are two potential safety hazards. The first of these, the problem of large numbers of cables on the floor, or dangling from the ceiling, is easy to tackle. Most offices need to tidy up their use of cables, and should see them as a hazard, both from the electrical viewpoint and from the risk of tripping over them.

The second, however, is that of VDU radiation emission. This is far from easy to tackle – largely because no-one seems able to agree whether or not there is radiation emission – there are very strong views on either side.

For example, a Canadian nuclear chemist, in a study on experiments in the administration departments in British Columbian hospitals (see *Fintech 2*, 14 August 1984) believes that low level radiation from VDUs could be the cause of failed pregnancies. His studies, however, showed the screens responsible to be over 8 years old.

In contrast, the manufacturers claim there is not enough scientific evidence for health hazard claims.

Nevertheless, if you are a user, it would be wise to offer any operators who fall pregnant the option of not working at a VDU, until, at least, the manufacturers are able to give adequate scientific evidence that there are no health risks.

Glossary

There are many glossaries on information technology, electronic office or office automation. The choice of this glossary is intended to cover the terms relevant to the user of office automation. Consequently, the reader will not find some of the more complicated technical terms in this glossary – they are best referred to in a technical handbook. However, we hope that in this glossary the reader will find the terms that either are, or will be, in relatively common usage by the users – the managers, and their staff whose jobs will be affected by office automation.

Abort Abandon work – either because of mistakes in data, or because of programming errors.

Access time Retrieval time for obtaining information from the storage medium.

Acoustic coupler A device to enable the connection of two pieces of computer equipment via a public telephone line, and, consequently, to pass information between the two.

Alphanumeric A set of characters that can contain combinations of letters, numbers and others such as punctuation marks.

Application software Programs written for a specific user application.

Archive To transfer information from on-line storage media eg RAMs to an off-line storage media eg floppy disks.

Architecture The formal structure by which various parts of an automated office can be interconnected.

Artificial intelligence Programs which enable computers to 'think' and 'reason' like a person would do, and to 'learn' from their 'experiences', incorporating them into its approach.

ASC II An American standard defining the storage and transmission of data.

Assembler The software that converts low level languages into machine code ie the language by which a machine operates.

Audio conferencing A meeting held in various locations, using voice communication (telephones) to connect the participants (possibly including facsimile).

Autodial The device that enables the automatic dialling of a prerecorded telephone number for connection to a computer. This provides the opportunity to retrieve information from remote machines using telephone lines at off peak costs.

Back-up Computing resources available in the event of the main system being faulty. (Also back-up copy for duplicate disks.)

Bandwidth Essentially, the amount of information that can be passed down a telecommunications link.

Bar code Thick and thin black lines acting as a representation of alphanumeric characters – the bar code system is used on consumer goods found in a supermarket.

Batch mode A computer operation in which transactions are inputted in batches, and processed one batch at a time.

BASIC A programming language used or available on many micros because of its simplicity – 'Beginners All-purpose Symbolic Instruction Code'.

Baud The measurement unit for the transmission of digital data over a telecommunications channel.

Binary The computing logic system – using a two state approach – either off/on, or yes/no, or 0/1 (the binary system).

Bit Binary digit – either 0 or 1.

Bps Bits per second.

Boilerplate The technique of merging standard, prerecorded text, with personalised text to assemble personalised documents.

Booting Using preliminary instructions to start up a computer system.

Broadband More than one device is able to use the same telecommunications link – 'broadband transmission'.

Bubble memory A solid state device enabling computer information to be stored on magnetic bubbles in a thin material film – the memory is not lost when power is turned off.

Buffer A memory which acts temporarily to compensate for the different speeds of communicating machines.

Byte 8 bits, representing the smallest memory the CPU can recall or store.

CAD Computer aided design.

CAL Computer aided learning.

CAM Computer aided manufacturing (often linked with CAD).

Carrier sensing The system used in a network to avoid the nodes trying to transmit simultaneously.

Cartridge Container holding magnetic disks and tapes.

Character A single letter, number, symbol or punctuation mark.

Chip The tiny piece of silicon on which the integrated electronic circuit is stamped.

Coaxial cable Cable used in transmitting communications, eg TV aerial cable – with 2 conductors inside, one insulated from the other.

COBOL A business orientated programming language.

Compatibility The ability of pieces of hardware to communicate with one another successfully and for software and data to be transmitted between each other.

Compiler A translator, converting user language programs and data into machine code.

Concurrency The ability of the operating system, eg concurrent CP/M-86, to undertake many tasks at the same time.

CP/M Control Program for Microprocessors – a commercial system (Digital Research), now an industry standard for operating systems for micros.

CPU Central processing unit – the logic system of a computer.

CRT Cathode ray tube – used in TV sets, and VDU screens – note: in USA, the VDU screens are called the CRT screen.

Cursor Movable marker on VDU screen.

Daisy wheel The type head for a daisy wheel printer – a fast letter quality printer – the head has print characters positioned at the end of spokes of a wheel (or petals of a daisy).

Database A collection of data which is inter-related so that chosen segments of it are easy to retrieve and store.

Data prep(aration) The clerical task of taking data in its raw form and preparing for subsequent input.

Debug Detection, location and correction of errors in a program.

Diagnostic Messages automatically produced by the computer to indicate and identify an error in a program or data.

Disk A method of storing data and text – magnetically coated materials on which digitized information can be stored – either *floppy* – a thin disk of plastic – or *hard* – a totally enclosed metal disk.

Disk drive The unit which reads to and from the disks.

Distributed processing A computer network with work stations (hence, processing) at many different locations (also known as *DDP – distributed data processing*).

Documentation The instruction manuals supplied with hardware and software.

Download To transfer information from an external device into a computer.

Downtime The amount of time hardware is out of operation because of a malfunction.

DOS Disk operating system – the sofware controlling the functioning of a disk drive. (MS–DOS and PC–DOS are commercial names).

Dot matrix A printer whose characters are formed by a combination of dots to produce the required letter or number. Not usually letter quality but the more dots, the better the quality.

Dumb terminal An on-line terminal which has neither memory nor CPU independent of its mainframe computer.

Dump To transfer bulk data or programs from one medium to another.

Editing Correcting, adding or moving around text or data to a program or memory.

Electronic mail/filing Using electronic transmission to send and receive messages and documents, and to file and retrieve such documents. Also includes the ability to store diaries and interrogate them to arrange meetings.

Electronic typewriter A typewriter with limited storage, editing and display facilities – can be updated to a word processor or connected to a PC.

End user The individual who operates the relevant part of a computer system.

Ergonomics The analysis of how people and machines work together.

Ethernet A commercial name for a local area network.

Expert system A computer system programmed to 'think' like a human being – usually on specific subjects (see also **artificial intelligence**).

External storage Any storage medium that is portable eg floppy disks.

Facsimile transmission FAX – transmitted whole images eg diagrams – from one loction to another.

Fibre optics Essentially a glass cable – telecommunications occur by pulsing light down bundles of continuous glass fibres.

Field An element of a record eg in a database.

File A collection of records which are logically related.

Floppy disk A soft, flexible plastic disk for storing data and text in a recorded magnetic form.

Font The type style and sizes a printer can produce with one instruction.

Full size display A VDU screen capable of showing a full A4 document – most screens are half page.

Gateway A link between one network and another eg teletex gateways between telex and personal computer.

GIGO Garbage in, garbage out – the quality of the information you get out is only as good as the quality of the information you put in.

Glare Excessive luminance caused by light from windows or lamps reflected off a terminal, which if incorrectly positioned causes eye strain.

Global exchange The ability to automatically change the same word or phase throughout a piece of text.

Graphics Pictures and diagrams represented on a VDU screen.

Handshaking   The exchange of predetermined signals as a control whenever a connection is established between two pieces of equipment.

Hard copy   Printed paper version of information.

Hard disk   An enclosed, rigid magnetic disk – with greater storage and faster access than a floppy.

Hardware   The physical equipment.

Host   The computer in a network providing the coordination facilities for the network, as well as providing services such as computation and database access (note: 'HOST' is also a commercial name for electronic mail software).

Housekeeping   The supporting operations – undertaken by the operator – that are secondary to main processing activities eg taking back-up copies, and maintaining file indices.

Icon/ikon   A screen symbol representing a particular function.

Impact printer   A printer where the images are created by the typehead hitting the paper eg daisy wheel.

Information centre   The centre in an organisation providing advice on office automation services.

Ink jet printer   A printer which creates images by squirting droplets of ink on to paper (a very high quality and very fast printer).

Integrated circuit   A solid state electronic microcircuit consisting of many components formed in miniature on a silicon chip.

Intelligent terminal   As opposed to a dumb terminal – this is an on-line terminal with its own CPU and memory independent of the mainframe.

Interactive   A system which enables the computer to interrogate the user and vice versa.

Interactive video   Using the new laser disk, this can be computer aided training or sales promotion, in which the communication with the user is via the video, and its progress and sequence is controlled by a micro and its software.

Interface   The point at which two systems or device come into contact with each other.

ISO   International Standards Organisation.

Justified text A facility on word processor software to ensure left and/or right margins are even.

Keypad An input device – usually with 10 digits and some control keys – used for data entry.

LAN Local area network.

Laser disk A new form of video, using laser technology to access information held on the disk rather than on a tape.

Laser printer A printer whose characters are created using lasers on light sensitive paper.

LCD Liquid crystal display – commonly used on calculators.

Letter quality Print acceptable for distribution outside an organisation.

Light pen A device shaped like a pen, which when moved over a screen allows the user to feed information to the computer – used for 'drawing' graphics.

LISP A commercial program capable of generating other programs – the beginnings of artificial intelligence.

Local area network A private system connecting devices within a small area.

Logging on/off The process of starting up a dialogue – usually with the provision of a password – and the terminating of the session.

LSI Large scale integration – chips containing a great number of integrated circuits (third generation of computers).

Machine code The binary code for the machine's basic instructions – which are directly acceptable to the CPU.

Mainframe A large computer – usually with many terminals attached.

Matrix printer (See **Dot matrix**.)

Megabyte A million bytes.

Menu A list of features available for the specific software (shown directly on the VDU).

Message switching A technique to enable a computer to receive and store a message, and wait until the recipient for whom it is intended is finally available and then transmitting it.

MICR   Magnetic ink character recognition – an input device for documents such as cheques where the characters and type-faces are printed in special ink.

Micro   A microcomputer.

Microfiche   Storage information in photographic sheets.

Mini   A minicomputer – larger than a micro, and capable of supporting terminals.

Mips   Million instructions per second – a measure of computing power.

MIS   Management information system – software which provides the required management information.

Modem   A device enabling the computer to be connected to a telecommunications network to communicate with other devices (*mo*dulator *dem*odulator).

Mouse   Device that can be rolled across a desktop causing the cursor to move in the same direction. Commonly used with icons- – when the cursor finds an icon, the user can push the button on the mouse, causing the computer to address the item referred to by the icon.

MS–DOS   A commercial name for a disk operating system.

Multiuser   A computer system capable of handling the requirements of many users concurrently.

Narrowband   Low capacity telecommunications channel.

Network   (See **LAN.**)

New technology agreements   Agreements reached with unions regarding the implementation of new technology.

Numeric keypad   (See **Keypad**).

OCR   Optical character recognition – an input device for reading text directly into an office automation system.

OEM   A company supplying systems, including components from another supplier.

Off/on line   Equipment that is *not connected/connected* directly to a computer for the purpose of processing.

Open systems   Networks deliberately built to standards which enable different types and makes of system to be interconnected.

Operating systems   The software that controls the operation of user programs.

Optical fibre (See **Fibre optics**.)

PABX Private automatic branch exchange – an internal telephone exchange – modern versions of which are computerised (previously called PBX when non-automated).

Packet switching A method of transmitting information over a network in individual 'packets' which have the relevant address information stored in the packet.

Paper tape An early form of input/output – punched paper tape.

Password A phrase (often personalised) to gain access to a computer system.

PC A personal computer – notably the IBM PC – essentially a microcomputer.

Peripheral 'Add-on' equipment to a CPU – eg disk drives, printers.

Phototypesetting A computer connected to a device enabling publication quality print to be produced for subsequent printing.

Pixel The smallest element of a VDU screen that can be individually addressed (or programmed for graphics purposes).

Plotter A computer controlled device to print graphics.

POS terminal Point of sale terminal eg terminals at checkouts in supermarkets.

Program A set of instructions to enable the machine to operate and carry out specific tasks.

Prompt A computer initiated message to cause the operator to progress to the next action.

Protocol Standards and format for communications between two devices.

PSTN Public switched telephone network – a wide area network.

QWERTY Standard typewriter keyboard layout.

RAM Random access memory – a memory for the use of recording transactions that are the subject of the current activity – the memory is lost when power is off, and can be written over in use.

Record A series of fields forming a complete piece of information eg name and address.

Realtime system A system which is 'live' and can respond instantly to queries or actions.

Report generator Software which enables outputs to be formatted in report format.

Resolution The degree to which the screen displays details – high resolution screens are necesary for graphics.

Response time The time a system takes to react.

Ring A network where each device is connected only to its two adjacent neighbours – hence messages have to pass through neighbours to get to another device.

ROM Read only memory – a permanent store of memory – not capable of being rewritten or written over.

Scroll To move text up and down on a screen.

Search and replace (See **Global exchange**.)

Semi-conductor Materials used in electronics eg silicon.

Shared facility Several pieces of equipment using the same facility eg common disk drives or shared printer.

Shared logic Workstations connected to a central computer providing the processing power.

Simulation Modelling the behaviour of one system using a computer.

Single line display The display used commonly for electronic typewriters and, more recently, lap size computers.

Soft copy Information displayed on a screen (cf hard copy).

Software Programs, procedures and routines concerned with operating a computer.

Speech recognition Identification of commands by a computer from an operator's spoken words.

Speech synthesis A computer producing simulated speech.

Split screen The ability to show more than one 'window' on a screen, showing different documents.

Spreadsheet An application program providing a grid for data which can then be manipulated.

Stand-alone An independent machine.

Standard text Text frequently used, that is stored and available for insertion into assembled documents.

Star   A network where each terminal is connected directly only to the central computer (cf **Ring**).

System disk   The disk holding the operating instructions program.

Tape   Used for input, output and storage (magnetic or paper).

Telecommunications   The transmission and reception of information by electronic or electrical means.

Teleconferencing   Meetings held with the participants linked by telephone lines.

Teletex   An international standard to enable machines to communicate *two way with each other* over public telecommunications networks.

Teletext   A link broadcasting information from a central source to receiving sets, such as TV sets, with special adaptors. Teletext is broadcast videotex, and popular applications include Oracle and Ceefax.

Telex   Still current – essentially electronic mail over a limited public network. Will be superseded when teletex becomes active.

Terminal   Device connected to a computer and capable of inputting and receiving output (see **Dumb** and **Intelligent**)

User friendly   A system designed to be used by operators without extensive computer training, and which has features to assist the user to operate the system.

UNIX   An operating system, currently receiving much interest and popularity, because of its ease of handling multiusers.

VDU   Visual display unit (also VDT – visual display terminal) – screen plus keyboard.

Video conferencing   A teleconference linking distant participants by *sound* and *vision*.

Videotex   The generic term for information broadcast from one central source to receiving sets–viewdata is interactive videotex and teletext is broadcast videotex.

Viewdata   Information transmitted to a user's TV set. The user can send simple messages to the system eg Prestel and 'home banking' – and thus the system is interactive.

Voice recognition   (See **Speech recognition**.)

WAN   Wide area network – the generic term for public

switched telephone network and other networks in development allowing communication between distant points.

Wideband   A communications link enabling a number of user communications.

Winchester disk   A hard disk enclosed in a hermetically sealed container.

Window   The VDU screen is split into sections enabling various sections of the memory (ie documents) to be observed at the same time.

Workstation   Any device which is provided for an individual to undertake electronic office work – usually combining keyboard, screen, processor and electronic mail.

Wraparound   Word processing jargon that indicates the software automatically starts a new line when it knows the next word in the text will reach the right-hand margin.

WYSIWYG   'What you see is what you get'. A term to indicate the system is able to reproduce screen graphics on a printer exactly. Particularly important when it comes to phototypesetting.

This glossary has been compiled and adopted from a number of sources: Wharton Publishing, *'A Glossary of Office Automation Terms'*, Henriques & Hoskins, *'How to Survive the Office of the Future'* Quiller Press.